MW01106730

The Princess Doll's Scrapbook

HER FAMILIES' EMIGRATION/ IMMIGRATION STORY

written by
Elaine Melby Ayre

Copyright © 2015 by Elaine Melby Ayre
First Edition – 2015

ISBN
978-1-77067-482-0 (Hardcover)
978-1-77067-483-7 (Paperback)
978-1-77067-484-4 (eBook)

All rights reserved.

No part of this publication may be reproduced in any form, or by any means, electronic or mechanical, including photocopying, recording, or any information browsing, storage, or retrieval system, without permission in writing from the publisher.

Produced by:

FriesenPress
Suite 300 –990 Fort Street
Victoria, BC, Canada V8W 3K2

www.friesenpress.com

Distributed to the trade by The Ingram Book Company

Contents

SOLO DEO GLORIA

Not to us, LORD, not to us, but to your name
be given glory on account of your gracious love and faithfulness.
Psalm 115:1

This book is dedicated
to
Maria's
Great-great-great
Grandchildren

Foreword

How could I have known the influence of Grandmother's simple gift? It was simple, yet complicated. The gift challenged me, demanding that the story be told of her life, as well as the lives and families of five generations of women and girls who had cherished this doll I named Princess.

The crush of pioneer life had taken its toll: Besides having her back shoulder broken off, she was a quadriplegic. Her original arms were missing, and the lower limbs were left as one-inch stubs. Haywire crisscrossing the body held the head on. A chemise of sorts, fashioned from old long underwear fabric, covered the original body. Tubes of crudely-fashioned pink muslin fabric replaced upper limbs. Nonetheless, the hauntingly beautiful face remained.

Our childhood dolls become a projection of ourselves, a focus of our hopes and dreams. Princess's own story journeyed to a time before her own creation, discovering her families, and the lives of women and daughters who cherished the doll.

"I believe dolls are the storytellers of the people and their heritage…"[1]

---

1   Marion E. Hislop, *Dolls in Canada* Dundern Press 1997 136 pp p12. Used with permission. This statement from Hislop's book *Dolls in Canada* inspired *The Princess Doll's Scrapbook.*

©CanstockPhotoInc/the poetic image
photoshopped by Marlene Atkinsen onto
Elaine Ayre's photograph of the doll

Part One
THE GIFT

Chapter One

LIFE WITH GRANDMA

Spending the summer of 1966, traveling around ten different European countries with my best friend, Jean, and other university friends had given me a taste of freedom. *Europe on $5 a Day* as our guidebook, opened up many varied and exciting opportunities. The final trip of the summer—the bus trip from Winnipeg to Estevan—seemed anticlimactic after that exciting two-month trip.

The day after my arrival, I would begin my new position as a home economics teacher at the Estevan Collegiate Institute. The previous year had been my first year of teaching in another southern Saskatchewan town where my doting landlady almost killed me with kindness. By the end of my stay there, I was itching to have my own place. Bursting with the need for independence, I went looking for my own apartment—but Grandma would not hear of it!

"But of course, you'll stay here with us," Grandma said, meaning with her and my single aunt, Evelyn, who lived here, too. Grandpa had passed away four years earlier, when I was away at university. Evelyn also was a teacher and had let me know about the position in Estevan; as a result, I now had the job.

Hence, my dreams of independence were curbed—yet in retrospect, it was timely; this afforded me the chance to spend time with my grandmother in her final years. She passed away after a brief period of hospitalization the spring of the second year I stayed with her. In this regard, being in her home was the opportunity of my lifetime.

At her insistence, I settled into the large upstairs bedroom with the big, street-view window, feeling quietly condescending at first. Yet having my turn to live in what had been my aunt's domain gave me a great deal of satisfaction. My grandfather was looking out for his four unmarried daughters when he first built this place and this was where they stayed when they were home for holidays. Two were married early, 1949 and 1952, and the remaining two never married so this would have been their home when they weren't away teaching. But Aunt Evelyn occupied the extra downstairs bedroom.

* * *

Years later, I received a copy of an article from the local newspaper, *Estevan Mercury*, reporting on a fire in what had been Grandma's house. The picture of firefighters on the porch roof seemed surreal; flames flickered outward from that very window where I used to sit to plan, sew or write letters. A flood of fond memories reminded me how significant those two years at my grandmother's had been.

In 1945, my grandparents moved from the farm they homesteaded in 1909, forty miles west of Estevan, to retire at the green and white stucco house they built at 1433 Third Street, Estevan. The Melby farm, my home, was three miles east of what had been my grandparents' homestead, but now we called that homestead, "Uncle's Place" because our uncles lived there.

Grandma and Grandpa, aunts and uncles, and cousins were a big part of my life. My mother was the oldest of a family of ten and the first one married, so I had four younger brothers before other cousins were born to vie for our grandparent's attention, though one more brother came after the cousin rush started in the early fifties. Altogether, there would be twenty-eight Hansen cousins.

SITTING ON THE BUMPER OF GRANDPA'S CAR

My brothers and I reveled in the attention. Picture three or four preschoolers perched on the truck's bench seat, hanging on to the dashboard (no seatbelts), going for a ride along with Uncle Johnny, or taking turns for a spin down the prairie trail with Uncle Lloyd on his new motor bike.

Or later, when I was older, I'd eavesdrop on the adult conversation from the top of the stairs when Uncle Bernhard or Clarence dropped by after bedtime.

I had more opportunities for getaways than my brothers did, staying at Grandma and Grandpa's on my own or visiting with aunts and uncles. My first train trip with Aunt Evelyn, when I was eight, was to see my first cousin, Vivian.

Being the oldest—and the only girl—created conflicting expectations for me. Sometimes I felt part of the older generation, when I was old enough to be a 'hired girl' on weekends and summer holidays as well as official babysitter for young cousins living nearby; I enjoyed the reward of earning a bit of money. At other times, I was Little Miss In-Between, feeling I didn't fit in anywhere. It didn't help that for the first half of my school life I had five boys in my grade to match my five brothers at home. But complete consolidation of rural school districts made grade eight [1955] a banner year for me. Finally, I had girls in my grade, some who became lifelong friends.

An example of conflicting expectations stands out in my memory: I had long dreamed for the opportunity to go to a Lutheran boarding school at Outlook for my grade twelve year. As I was settling in to dorm life, a letter from my grandfather dampened my excitement. He had seen me wearing lipstick at a friend's wedding in Estevan several weeks before. His letter expressed strong disapproval and disappointment.

I was to be an example for all of my younger cousins, and painted lips was not the way God made me! Grandpa's strict code of living forbade things he viewed as worldly, like drinking liquor, smoking, dancing, and wearing makeup or high-heeled shoes and fancy jewelry, especially earrings. Yet, I thought, pictures I'd seen of Billy Graham's wife, someone Grandpa had the utmost respect for; though they were in black and white, the photographs definitely indicated she was wearing makeup.

* * *

Needlework, knitting and sewing were Grandma's main pastimes. On my sixth birthday she gave me a framed embroidered picture she made of the bedtime prayer, "Now I lay me down to sleep"—a treasured keepsake.

> At that time, farming newspapers like *The Western Producer* were sources for craft and sewing patterns ordered by mail, such as the embroidery transfer used to create the picture grandma gave me and ten years later a nature scene I stitched for myself. The material used was the ever-present sugar or flour sack, recycled into dishtowels, pillowcases, clothing or decorative items, like my picture. The dish towels of today don't begin to compare with those of

yesterday that started out as a hundred pound flour or sugar sack.

Shortly after this, Grandma gave me a cellophane bread bag stuffed with fabric scraps and a piece of paper outlining various quilt patterns. Choosing a flattened diamond shape, I used a cornflakes box to make a stencil to trace around. Then, I cut six pieces for my first hand-sewn quilt block. Sewn together, they produced a hexagon (Mum finished the hexagon quilt for me fifteen years later when I returned to university after living at my grandmother's).

Graduating to the treadle machine was the next step. Mum eventually got an electric one when rural electrification came to our farm in the early fifties. She put that sewing machine to good use, turning out five sets of flannelette pajamas and snappy sport shirts yearly for her crew of five boys, as well as special dress outfits for me. After practicing on simple projects, I was soon interested in making my own clothes.

The quilt Grandma introduced me to, was made up of a collection of materials from grandma's aprons and dresses and all the clothes Mother made for my brothers, herself and me, as well as many I made for myself through the teen years. Grandmother's bag of scraps and my mother's good taste in clothes eventually influenced my choice of study—a degree and teaching career in Home Economics.

***

Living in Estevan those two years was a one-of-a-kind opportunity. I got to know my grandmother on an adult level. Macular degeneration had severely impaired Grandma's vision, and bone cancer—an aftermath of the breast cancer she suffered in the 1930s—impacted her later years, yet she never complained. Although she said she could not imagine any more changes in the world, she just went on about life as usual.

I always came home for lunch; Grandma prepared it. After we ate, she washed and I dried the dishes. Estevan Collegiate was only a few blocks from her house—therefore, she and I had time, one-on-one, five days a week, as my aunt always took her lunch. The school where she taught was across busy railroad tracks on the other side of town.

Now Grandma's 'fancy work' was knitting square dishcloths out of cotton string provided by the Canadian National Institute for the Blind. Though the strands were thick, she still needed our help to pick up dropped stitches. CNIB supplied a talking book machine, sending out big and bulky tapes by mail, before cassette players became common. Grandma spent many hours in the green side chair listening to these recorded books.

One of Grandma's stories revealed they had not always been so strict in their practices, for there had been dancing at the housewarming party in celebration of the completion of their new house in 1919. She told me a quarrel had erupted between their neighbours, who lived a mile southwest. The husband, a very sociable type, had a great time dancing with the younger women, while his much-older wife developed a case of severe jealousy. Grandma's story surprised me; I could not imagine this incident happening at Grandma's house!

**

The two-room homestead shack that had been Grandpa and Grandma's accommodation up till then was definitely overcrowded, for there was Edith (1910), Myrtle (1911), Bernhard (1913), Clarence (1915), Anna (1917), and Clara (1918). Since lodging was often required for a hired man or a hired girl, in addition to their family, imagine how welcome the new two-story home with four bedrooms upstairs was?

A Mission-style rocker and chair set was the community's gift at this housewarming celebration. (I'm not sure what happened to the chair, but the rocker ended up in my possession after the birth of my second son.)

Five more were born in the new house in the twenties: Evelyn (born in 1921, died 1922),

Johnny (1923), Evelyn (1925), Lloyd (1926) and Palmer (1929). Four plus six equal ten children.

***

One day, in the early spring of 1967, a friend dropped me off in front of Grandma's house for the lunch break. Parked on the street was my very own car, a red Valiant, my pride and joy, recently acquired from my uncle Bernhard. A barely visible patch of ice, formed from snow melting off the car, took my feet out from under me. I picked myself up and went inside.

Grandma was sitting in her rocker, waiting with lunch for me. With my heart pounding, I sat on the chair, breathlessly telling her what happened. Tears immediately welled up in her eyes; her concern was that I might be badly hurt, though I did not think I was. Her depth of emotion moved me—normally our family did not express much emotion.

At 3:30, following my afternoon classes, I went to the clinic down the street. Several days later, after technicians read the x-rays, I learned that I had a compression fracture of the ninth dorsal vertebrae. A body cast was to be my shell for three months.

***

After lunch one day, before the cast episode, as we sat at the gray Arborite kitchen table. Grandma left the room and returned holding an old shoebox. She handed it to me, saying simply, "Here, I'd like you to have this."

I lifted the lid. There, like a body in a coffin, resting on ivory satin fabric scraps, was Grandma's doll.

The doll had seen better days—her striking face, however, was still beautiful. Though I realized it was special to Grandma, I didn't think too much of it at the time.

In the early fifties, that doll sat on the guest room bed with a blue 'milk filter' outfit covering her stubs of legs. This craft used circular milk filters joined with knotted yarns to create a bubble-style skirt, meant for an 8-inch craft doll. Since this doll was meant to be taller, the outfit's proportions didn't suit her. I removed that milk filter outfit to find the body covered with a sewn-on wrapper made from heavy cotton underwear fabric.

* * *

Grandma, in her shy, unassuming way, did not offer any explanation. Many times, I wished I'd asked questions. I wondered:

What happened to the doll's shoulder, arms, legs, and her jewelry?

How was she dressed?

Who gave her to you?

What had this doll meant to you when you were growing up?

Did I even say thank you?

Finding answers became my lifelong quest. Meanwhile, the doll did not decay in her shoebox coffin. Every once in a while I took the doll out and asked myself, *"Is restoration possible?"*

Chapter Two

THE RESTORATION

In subsequent years, the doll was close by, hidden away on a high closet shelf, resting on ivory satin. Occasionally, I took the doll down to show to a friend or to reflect on what I might do to improve her situation.

After those two years at my grandmother's place, I experienced many life changes— further education, moves, marriage, children, and work.

Fast forward twelve years to 1980; we had been back in our Northwest Calgary home five years. Our son was seven. Plans to take a trip to Europe had progressed as far as getting passports and plane tickets. I was looking forward to enjoying the sights of Europe again, this time with my husband, Gary, and son, William.

The infamous Calgary Teacher's Strike of 1980 threatened, starting at the end of May. With our family's two teacher incomes in jeopardy, we realized we hadn't saved enough to back up our trip. Early resolution of the strike seemed unlikely, so we cashed in our plane tickets. The strike stretched on until October when a contract settlement allowed us to go back to work.

***

Although disappointing, cancelling the trip to Europe was a smart decision and provided a unique prospect for the doll and me.

With time on my hands, I checked the Yellow Pages for a place to buy the missing parts for my doll. The doll and I visited a porcelain doll maker who lived close by. I selected what I thought were appropriate arms and feet.

The doll maker's enthusiasm overshadowed my selection process. That very weekend, she was offering an ambitious porcelain doll-making workshop. Her passion was contagious. With nothing else pressing, except for the occasional requirement to walk picket lines, I signed up.

That weekend, a small group of soon-to-be doll makers met in her basement workshop. Preparing the greenware pieces, arranged in advance by pouring porcelain slurry (called slip) into molds began the painstaking process.

That amounted to twelve pieces, for we were making a fully-jointed porcelain doll with glass eyes that opened and shut, as well as creating a wig. It was an ambitious project. This doll was a copy of an Armand Marseilles doll, crafted by a well-known French doll-making company from the later 1800s, similar to the Shirley Temple doll of the 1930s, or an early Eaton's "Beauty Doll" of the same period.

"Baby Betty" was the second doll. Despite her name, she did not have baby-like features—she was small, at only ten inches tall. She had five porcelain pieces, a head (or bust) attached to a stuffed fabric body, and hands and boots tied to fabric limbs—the basic construction of Grandma's doll. Both dolls are shown on the next page on the quilt Grandma got me started on.

The process of working with the greenware included smoothing out ridges where the two halves of the mold met, and sanding until the surface was smooth as silk. Firing the pieces in the kiln changed the gray clay to a slightly rosy skin tone. Now the pieces were not so fragile. On the second day, we started the painstaking task of colouring the features.

To begin making a wig, we shaped a piece of horsehair canvas over a Styrofoam ball that was the same diameter as the head. Then we took apart an artificial hair wig, strand by strand, stitching it onto the base until there was complete miniature head of hair. The instructor demonstrated the basics of the process we completed later on our own. Work, such as setting the eyes or the teeth, or stringing the doll together required additional visits to the workshop to complete. Now I

ELAINE MELBY AYRE

understood why the price of a handmade porcelain doll was hundreds of dollars.

Period dolls must be dressed in styles and materials authentic to their time. No polyester or other synthetic fiber allowed. For petticoats and pantaloons, cotton lawn, a soft, fine fabric was selected. The choice for the dress was a crisp, sheer cotton organdy. Since organdy only came in white, I hand dyed the fabric.

The smaller doll was going to model a *bunad* (Norwegian regional costume) with a fine wool navy skirt, white blouse, beaded hat, belt, and plastron and red vest, just like the one my mother received when her father returned from a trip to Norway in 1926. That is still the plan!

That weekend workshop grew into weeks of work, but doll making is play for grownup doll lovers! The Calgary Teacher's Strike of 1980 gave me the special opportunity of uninterrupted time for which I am ever grateful; it allowed circumstances to work together so I could make those two porcelain dolls, and learn how to restore Grandma's precious doll.

With the old body covering removed, I could see the original sawdust-filled body of sturdy pink twill fabric was very clean, considering the doll's age. However, the haywire crisscrossing the body, which had held the head on for countless decades, had formed deep rust stains. With the wire removed, the head bust was detached from the body and sent to a "Doll Hospital" where the broken shoulder was reconstructed. With the back and shoulder built up, I could hardly tell the right shoulder was not original.

Copying what I had done to make the "Baby Betty" doll, I restored Grandma's doll, making new fabric limbs and attaching the purchased porcelain hands and boots. Now I wished I hadn't been in such a hurry to purchase the missing limbs. I should have chosen hands with finer, more careful detailing—for how many times had the instructor insisted I start a detail over in order to get it just right?

Back when I lived at Grandma's place, a doll supply catalogue chart informed me: this doll should be nineteen and a half inches tall, based on the head circumference. The doll's stub legs required an extension before attaching the black high top boots to reach that height. I pushed the porcelain foot inside the fabric tube "leg" until the ridge above the "boot" lined up. Strong linen cord tied the porcelain limb to the fabric limb. Then it was turned right side out, stuffed, and attached to the body. I recognized the link between the porcelain and the fabric as a weak point in a much-played-with doll. And if the porcelain limb came off, the sawdust stuffing would spill out. This possibly explained the doll's short stub legs and missing arms.

Grandma's doll needed no wig, for she had a finely-detailed molded hairstyle. With a blonde braid circling her head like a crown, topped off with a fan of ringlets, she looked like a Norwegian princess.

ELAINE MELBY AYRE

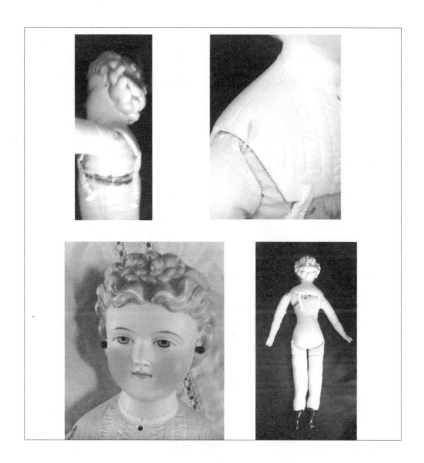

I made the dress for Grandma's doll by hand, using vintage materials. With no idea what her original clothing was, I thought it appropriate to dress her in a reproduction of the bridal dress my grandmother had made and worn for her March 25, 1909 wedding. Fifty years later, I modelled that dress for Grandma and Grandpa's wedding anniversary celebration in March 1959. At 16, I was the family member closest to Grandma's size when she was married.

The style featured a shirtwaist top with full sleeves, long buttoned cuffs, a high neck, decorated yoke, and gathered skirt with three deep tucks and a shaped waistband. The fine ivory wool challis fabric I found was almost the same as the original.

WEDDING PORTRAIT
JOHN AND DINA HANSEN
MARCH 25, 1909

ELAINE MELBY AYRE

GRANDPARENTS ENJOYING THEIR SPECIAL DAY

50ᵀᴴ WEDDING ANNIVERSARY PICTURE WITH ELAINE
WEARING HER GRANDMOTHER'S WEDDING DRESS

Ten years before the teacher's strike, I had been teaching in Fort Simpson, NWT, sixteen hundred or more miles away from my home and planning my own wedding. I wrote to Aunt Evelyn requesting a picture of that dress so I could recreate style features of Grandmother's wedding dress for my own. The old oval-framed wedding portrait with curved glass meant photocopying was not possible. On a Sunday afternoon visit, several younger cousins drew pictures showing the fashion details of Grandma's wedding dress. These were mailed to me. Referencing those drawings a decade later, I recreated the dress in miniature.

Ideas and style features for making pantaloons and a petticoat came from studying turn-of-the-century mail-order catalogues. How interesting it was to see the kinds of undergarments women wore in the late 1800s and early 1900s! Since bodice detailing was engraved onto the porcelain, I didn't bother with a chemise, the article of clothing meant to cover the upper torso.

Except for recreating a lace effect on the yoke using fancy pattern stitches on my sewing machine, the dress was completely hand-stitched.

***

Now I look at that special portrait, the doll reminds me of Grandma Dina. Forty years later the oval framed tinted wedding photo of my grandparents is on my wall, above the doll on the corner cabinet my husband built just for her.

The doll with rosy cheeks is forever the blushing bride, contradicting untold stories of unspoken hard times. The satin stuffed shoebox is gone. Proudly displayed is the resurrected doll.

She needed a name. Since she looked like a Norwegian princess—and since Princess is often used as a term of endearment—I even thought that Grandma, as a young girl might have called her that. Considering my grandmother was born in 1887, I knew Princess was old. She was a precious keepsake to remind and connect me to a heritage from days gone by. Her story was a mystery to me, but I would take baby steps to unravel that story Princess had to share.

Chapter Three

SEEDS OF A STORY

"We were hard up so didn't have as nice clothes as some of our neighbours so we didn't go out much. And I didn't go to school before I was thirteen years old."

Sometime in the early nineteen sixties, my grandmother wrote this in a short two-page account about her early life. Her story confirmed that Grandma hadn't gone to school until she was thirteen, because her family couldn't afford shoes.

But, if Grandma's family was that poor, how could they buy a doll as fine as this one? That puzzled me.

Grandmother's oldest brother, Jens Gronvold, had written a four-page chronicle telling his mother and father's story sometime in the mid-sixties, a short time before he died. A clue, along with a gut feeling, jumped out. Reading between the lines became the starting point for this doll's story.

Many times, I felt the gift of the doll was an encumbrance—another burden of responsibility. I should not keep her to myself; I had to find a way to learn and share her story.

Eight years after completing Princess's restoration, I drafted my original three-page "doll's story" to use for a special 1988 Christmas letter for my family. This way, my aunts, uncles and cousins could share in the unfolding tale of the doll Grandmother had given me twenty years earlier.

Jens's chronicle started in 1869 when Grandma's mother, Maria, immigrated to America from Norway with her sister, Karine, and their much younger brother, Laurits.

Maria had a married sister, Bertha, living near Decorah, Iowa, who she helped, especially during the busy times such as harvest season. Otherwise, she worked as a housekeeper in at least two households, including the home of the editor of the well-known Norwegian newspaper, *Decorah Posten*. In one of those households, the wife died; the widower would have married Maria but, Jens wrote, Maria "preferred Johan from the store".

A germ of an idea grew from reading between the lines. I had a feeling that the doll was older than my grandmother, even if I had no proof. Was there a link between this doll, the store, and the Johan Gronvold, who Maria eventually married?

Four girls central to the doll's story were revealed: Jenny and Nelly, the twin daughters of Maria's sister Bertha, born in 1867, my grandmother, Dina, born in 1887, and her older sister, Ragna, born in 1877, halfway between. But Ragna died in 1889 when Dina was only a year old. I believed these four first-generation Norwegian-American girls, spaced a decade apart, along with Maria (and Johan's courtship), were linked with this doll. I felt I knew something of their life and times based on the fact that Laura Ingalls Wilder, author of *Little House on the Prairie*, shared the twin's birth year; my grandmother shared the same birth year as that of Laura's daughter, Rose Wilder.

My theory was that Maria visited the store where her brother Hans worked, saw the doll, then met Johan, a more recent newcomer. Both the doll and Johan caught her eye; she then bought the doll to give to her twin nieces. Maria, a twin herself, probably felt a special connection to these little girls and became a doting aunt to them.

***

Though I was convinced this doll was older than my grandmother was, finding proof seemed impossible. Porcelain dolls often have a distinguishing mark at the back of the head, neck or back. Unfortunately, that was the part broken off in this particular doll. The desired reference point was gone.

On many occasions, I sneaked peeks at doll books in bookstores or checked out antique doll websites, spending countless hours going through as many as seventy-five pages of antique dolls listed on EBay. Never did I find a doll that resembled mine—and I took pride in the fact that none of them were as beautiful as Princess.

My doll's origin remained a complete mystery until 2007 when I went to see a doll-maker in Airdrie.

She said, "I'm not sure, but I think it is an 1870 German Parian doll."

On my return home, I googled "1870 German Parian doll" and found there an online preview section of a recently published book titled *Identifying German Parian Dolls* by Mary Gorham Krombholz. This doll was from 1870. Here was proof for my theory. After all the years of wondering, I was overjoyed.

Identical big 'sisters' of my doll were pictured on page forty-one (in illustrations 30, 31 and 32). One had a six-and-a-half-inch head, and the other a six-inch head. I grabbed a tape measure to check Princess: my doll's head was four-and-a-half inches. Measuring the doll's head was how I determined that she should be 19 ½ inches tall.

The doll "…has typical factory facial features which include blue painted eyes, finely outlined in black, a tiny white iris highlight on the left side of each iris and a V-shaped darker-red lip accent line. The shoulder plate is pierced below the neckline to hold a piece of coral."[2]

According to Krombholz, these facial details are characteristic of dolls made by the Alt, Beck and Gottschalk Company.

"The shoulder plate contains alternating cross-stitched and gathered bodice details. The upswept blonde hair is styled in braids that encircle the head and form a semi-circle in front."[3]

***

---

2   Mary Gorham Krombholz *Identifying German Parian Dolls* Reverie Publishing 2006 160 pp Used with permission

3   Mary Gorham Krombholz *Identifying German Parian Dolls* Reverie Publishing 2006 160 pp Used with permission

My gut feeling was right! The doll was seventeen years older than my grandmother was. So, it was entirely possible that Great-Grandmother Maria purchased the doll to give to her twin nieces, Jenny and Nelly, sometime before she was married. After all, she'd been in America seven years before her marriage. My guess was that she bought the doll in October 1873, when the twins were six.

The doll that Maria selected from the store in Decorah, Iowa originated in the Thuringian area of eastern Germany. Besides porcelain dolls, the Thuringian region is known for many World Heritage sites as well as famous, influential men, such as Martin Luther, Johann Sebastian Bach, Frederick Schiller, Goethe, and Franz Liszt.

At least ten different doll-making companies operated in the forested Thuringian region of east central Germany in the latter nineteenth century, among them Alt, Beck and Gottschalk. Clay mined here was suitable for porcelain. I wasn't able to determine if completed dolls were made there, or if the parts were shipped, then completed with bodies— and subsequently dressed in clothing—once exported to the United States.

> *Parian* type porcelain is white and has a matte unglazed finish. The word "parian" refers to a kind of marble from the island of Paros.

> *China* has white base porcelain and coated with a shiny glaze. *Bisque* is unglazed but tinted— generally in a pink tone for dolls.

***

My curiosity about my Princess doll's story ordained me to research Great-Grandmother Maria's family. Our family had a history written in Norwegian of our Grandpa J.B. Hansen's family. We referred to it as *The Blue Book* because we couldn't say its Norwegian name; it was published in the early 1960s, several years before my grandfather, JB Hansen, died.[4] *The Blue Book* thoroughly informed us about the paternal branch of my family. But as was typical of the time, Maria—known to the world as Mrs. Johan Gronvold—gave few answers as to the what, when, where, who, why and how of her family.

The doll and her story became the force for uncovering and gathering a comprehensive family and immigration history I envisioned as *The Princess Doll's Scrapbook*.

***

I first learned about Great Grandmother Maria's area of old Norway when Lillehammer was host city for the XVII Winter Olympics in 1994. Lillehammer is the capital city of the Oppland region of central Norway. Oppland was Maria's original home county and where she emigrated from to start a new life in North America. Thus, we travel back to look at her families' histories.

---

4   Broder Jordbraek *The Chronicles of the Ancient Family of Skoger* Translation by Hans Anders Skjeldrum Elgvang, 2011. I received a copy of an English translation of *The Blue Book* from this distant cousin of mine. Broder, responsible for the original book, was my grandfather's youngest brother.

Part Two
HER FAMILIES' HISTORIES

Chapter Four

KALEIDOSCOPE OF
NORSK KULTUR

Without a glimpse into the kaleidoscope of Norwegian culture that was the background of her families, Princess's scrapbook would be incomplete.

I was proud of my Norwegian heritage. My parent's first language had been Norwegian and their speech always held traces of its singsong accent. They spoke Norwegian when they visited with my grandparents or other old-timers and to each other when they wanted to "hide" what they were saying from us children.

My grandparent's accent was even stronger. If we were riding in Grandpa's car, we almost burst with stifled laughter when Grandma announced from the front seat, "Vaall...hare ve arr... back on Turd Street," as Grandpa turned left off Souris Avenue onto Third Street.

Unfortunately, any attempt to teach us Norwegian did not go much beyond the perfectly polite exclamation of disgruntlement, "*Uffda*." One source described "*Uffda*" as equivalent to Charlie Brown's "Good Grief."

We did learn the first verse of the Christmas carol "I Am So Glad Each Christmas Eve" so we could sing it for Grandma and Grandpa.

Jeg er så glad hver julekveld,
for da ble Jesus født,
da lyste stjernen som en sol,
og engler sang så søtt.

I am so glad each Christmas Eve,
The night of Jesus' birth!
Then like the sun the Star shone forth,
And angels sang on earth.[5]

The little Child in Bethlehem,
He was a King indeed!
For he came down from heaven above
To help a world in need

He dwells again in heaven's realm,
The Son of God today;
And still he loves his little ones
And hears them when they pray.

I am so glad on Christmas Eve!
His praises then I sing;
He opens then for every child
The palace of the King.

* * *

Though our Grandpa was not a good singer, he was never shy about sharing a song of faith at any gathering. But this song was his way of interacting with the youngest ones from his brood of over two dozen grandchildren. He sat with his knees crossed, placed the youngster on his foot, held the baby's hands and sang this as he gave a bouncy ride on

---

5   Words: Inger M. Wexelsen, 1859; translated from Norwegian to English by
     Peter A. Sveeggen, 1931. Marie Wexelsen (1832-1911) published three chil-
     dren's books, among them Ketil, en Julegave for De Smaa (Ketil, a Christmas
     Gift for Little Ones), where this song introduced a longer story. At that time she
     entitled it "The Child's Christmas Carol."

ELAINE MELBY AYRE

his foot. This playful riding song "*Ride Ride Ranke*" (pronounced Reeda Reeda Runka) was one I remembered. The words tell about a child riding to Grandfather's (*Bestefar*) house[6].

> *Ride, ride ranke!*
> *Si meg hvor skal veien gå?*
> *Bestefar besøk skal få.*
> *Ride, ride ranke!*

Riding riding upright
Tell me, where does the road lead to (where are we riding)?
Grandad will get a visit (we will visit Grandad)
Riding riding upright

Once we were too old for the ride, Grandpa's treat came from the peppermint jar kept in the middle cupboard.

***

We celebrated Christmas on Christmas Eve, which is the Norwegian custom, along with our Grandma and Grandpa, aunts, uncles, and cousins. And each year, a different family took their turn to host the festivities, and everyone contributed to the menu.

Various Norwegian delicacies were part of the menu. There was *lutefisk* (translated lye fish), boiled in an improvised cheesecloth bag in a pot of water and served with melted butter. The distinct odour of the

---

6   http://barnesanger.wikispaces.com/Ride,+ride+ranke — gives various versions from Denmark, Sweden and Norway. This version was how my grandfather sang it, slightly different than the musical notation given on this website. Four or five verses take the ride to Grandma, uncles and aunts, but I only remember hearing this first verse.

steamy fish prevailed over the wonderfully rich aroma of the turkey, golden brown and awaiting carving. *Lutefisk*, with its jelly-like texture, was an acquired taste. One either loved or hated it.

The youngsters favored the assortment of baked goods more than that slightly sweet dark brown goat cheese (*gjetost*—pronounced "yay-toast") which Aunt Myrtle brought every year.

Within a few short hours after dinner, the coffee pot went on, to accompany another round of sweets. The trays might include *Krumkake*, *Berlinerkranser*, *Peperkaker*, and *Lefse*

Krumkake are thin pancakes baked on a special patterned grill and rolled into a cone while still hot. The name literally means "crumb cake", since they are so crumbly. They remind me of a small delicate version of a waffle cone, meant to be served filled with cream or fruit. They are a special treat for the Christmas season. We usually had them plain.

Berlinerkranser or Berlin Wreaths are delicate-tasting butter cookies shaped like a wreath. I remember rolling out chunks of dough into pencil-like tubes, then twisting them into wreaths, painting the tops with egg white, and sprinkling with coarse sugar before baking them.

Pepperkaker look like gingerbread, but pepper and spices make them brown, not molasses.

Our all-time favorite was *lefse*, thin tortilla-like bread made with boiled mashed potatoes and butter or lard and flour. For authentic *lefse*, a special carved rolling pin is used. Then a long carved wooden *lefse* stick, like an extra-long spatula, rolls up the rather delicate *lefse* to transfer it gently onto the surface of the hot grill where it is gently unrolled. When it is freckled and brown, it is turned. When little air pockets appear, press down gently. Transfer the cooked *lefse* to a clean flat toweled surface to cool. Serve it buttered and sprinkled with sugar, preferably brown, along with cinnamon, rolled up tightly and cut into portions.

Don't set it out too soon, for the youngsters have been known to sneak a piece or two for a pre-dinner snack!

***

Elaine Melby Ayre

A command performance, especially for Grandma and Grandpa, took place after the meal and before the gift opening. Children performed songs or recitations learned for their Christmas programs at school and Sunday school.

I remember 1952, the year the group gathered at our Melby place, our newest uncle, Olaf, took a picture of Grandma and Grandpa surrounded by nine grandchildren, each holding up the gift received from Grandma and Grandpa and Aunt Myrtle and Evelyn. I was nine years of age; I secretly thought I was too old for the most beautiful doll—but it was as pretty as the neighbour girl's doll, which I'd quietly coveted for a long time.

* * *

In 1955, our aunts, Myrtle and Evelyn, spent several months in Norway, connecting with our Norwegian roots. In preparation for this visit our grandpa arranged for a family portrait to give to his family back in Norway.

Souvenirs aside, the personal connection Myrtle and Evelyn initiated lasted over fifty years. It was the most important gift they gave me from this trip. They introduced me to a Norwegian pen pal, my second cousin from Kongsberg, Norway. Bjorg, who was my age (twelve), had started to study English in school; she practiced by writing letters to me. We met in person for the first time that summer of 1966 when I travelled with friends through Europe, before I moved into Grandmother's house. Since then, she and her husband have visited back and forth many times. On one of those more recent times, we met at an Alberta cousin's reunion. I introduced her to Grandma's Princess doll.

Chapter Five

KALEIDOSCOPE EXTENDED

In those busy days and years before Princess Doll's restoration, I experienced a number of memorable summers working as a cook for the Trollhaugen Language Arts and Cultural Camp.[7] During a weeklong event, campers participated in many aspects of Norwegian arts and culture, including classes in language, music, crafts, and folk dancing. Like the prospect to learn porcelain doll making, this opportunity fell into my lap and proved to be providence.

In 1974, my husband and I spent the month of July at the Mulhurst Lutheran Bible Camp; a summer cooking job there gave us a welcome working holiday, for it had been a busy year—my first year back teaching after maternity leave, while my husband spent his first year at university working part-time.

The camp manager called us and asked, "Would you come back for the third week of August when the Norwegian Camp is being hosted? The August cook can't stay."

This was a surprise—and we agreed; it sounded like fun! After that initial week in August, spending the third week in August at the camp became a part of our summer for fifteen years.

***

Starting with the first day, we experienced many aspects of Norwegian culture. For the official camp opening, the Norwegian flag was raised

---

7   Trollhaugen was a project of Sons of Norway Lodges in Alberta

along with a make-believe celebration of Norwegian Independence Day (after being under Danish rule for some 400 years, Norway instituted a special day—May 17, 1814—when a constitutional convention declared Norway a free and indivisible kingdom. Union with Sweden did continue until 1905, when Norway finally achieved independence).

Campers young and old paraded, waving miniature paper Norwegian flags as they do at *Syttende Mai* (Seventeenth of May) celebrations in Norway. Harry led the procession playing traditional tunes on his Hardanger fiddle. Those who knew the words sang the Norwegian National anthem, as the Norwegian flag was raised.

Ja, Vi Elsker Dette Landet (Yes, We Love This Land)[8]

Ja, vi elsker dette landet,
som det stiger frem,
furet, værbitt over vannet,
med de tusen hjem.
Elsker, elsker det og tenker
på vår far og mor
og den saganatt som senker
drømmer på vår jord.
og den saganatt som senker
senker drømmer på vår jord.

Translation (metrical version)
Norway, thine is our devotion,
Land of hearth and home,
Rising storm-scarr'd from the ocean,
Where the breakers foam.
Oft to thee our thoughts are wending,
Land that gave us birth,
And to saga nights still sending
Dreams upon our earth,
And to saga nights still sending
Dreams upon us on our earth.

---

8   http://en.wikipedia.org/wiki/Norwegian_national_anthem

                           ELAINE MELBY AYRE

A Hardanger fiddle (or in Norwegian, *Hardangerfele*) is often called the national instrument of Norway. It is like a violin, but is made of much thinner wood, often highly decorated with mother of pearl inlays and drawn patterns on the top. An extra set of sympathetic strings gives a drone-like quality to the music.

***

The most unforgettable theme day was the celebration of Old Norse Heritage—a Viking-style meal where the only eating tool allowed was a knife. Forks and spoons, as eating tools, hadn't yet been developed in Viking times (though I've been told they did have wooden spoons). The Norwegian cooking class made crisp flatbread. We broke it off in small pieces to scoop up chunks of *lapskaus* or stew.

The dining room setup represented a long Viking hall. Two fellows played the roles of famed Vikings, Leif Erickson, and his son, Eric the Red; others played their anonymous cohorts. They sat at the front while girls in Viking-style dress served their every beck and call. It was great fun to play Vikings!

Earlier that afternoon, a play reenacted the Vikings' meeting with the Indians at L'Anse Aux Meadows, the site of a Viking Village at the head of Newfoundland's Great Northern Peninsula. Here the Vikings settled for a short time in Northern Newfoundland, five centuries before Columbus discovered the New World. They called this place Vinland.

The discovery of this site did not happen until the 1960s. Now, Parks Canada preserves the Viking village ruins as a UNESCO World Heritage Site—a monument to early Viking explorers and a matter of great pride for those, like me, interested in all things Norwegian.

Early accounts of Viking discoveries, including their discovery of North America, came from the Greenlander and Vinlander sagas. These sagas were ancient Norse stories told by word of mouth for many years, and later written down for future generations to read. Ancient Norse runic writing was an angular type of script inscribed on wood or stone. The earliest written versions of many of the sagas date back to the twelfth century. What remains of this early Old Norwegian language is the language spoken today in Iceland.

The Latin alphabet and language changes to Norway came about after Saint Olaf (1016-1030) Christianized Norway. Wooden churches built in the medieval period are stave churches, a unique form of construction that lasted many centuries. Currently, around two dozen of these structures remain, protected as world heritage sites.

***

After the Black Death—a plague that affected much of Europe in the 1300s—ran its course through Norway, many farms lay idle. Since there was a lack of real leadership, Denmark took over the governing of the country. The Danish language had a strong effect on language in Norway over that 400-year period.

***

At the beginnings of independence and the Norwegian renaissance, a language movement called *Nynorsk* developed. The intention was to make the Norwegian less like the Danish. My distant cousin, Philip reported that his Norwegian immigrant father had trouble reading letters and papers he received from Norway because the language had changed so much from what he'd been taught as a boy in the 1880 to 1890 period. Another example of language changes: the name of my ancestor, Paul Skarie, was spelled three different ways in the records: Paal, Povel, and Paul.

To complicate matters, each valley had a distinctive dialect.

Philip provided this example:

"When I was an infant, a young woman from Bergen helped Mother. My father, who came from Skjåk in Gudbrandsdalen, and the young woman from Bergen could not understand each other's Norwegian.

Mother, who studied Norwegian in college, had to translate for the two native Norwegians."[9]

Not surprising, then, when Norwegian linguists studied the old language, they did so among the many Norwegian settlements in America.

* * *

A mythical theme repeated every camp season was a celebration of *trolls* and *nisse* and other fairy-type folk. You might know that most familiar Norwegian folktale "The Three Billy Goats Gruff." Each time the billy goats passed over the bridge to get to their pasture of green grass, a nasty old troll living under it challenged them.

Gigantic troll heads, scarier than Shrek, made of papier-mâché, were part of the interesting store of resources put together by dedicated individuals from the Trollhaugen Language Arts and Cultural Association.

Some older boys played trolls, by wearing those "heads." They ran in and out of the bushes, while campers gathered around a large campfire as a celebration of St Hans Fest or *Jonsokdag*. In Norway this is Saint John the Baptist Day, which falls on the longest day, the first day of the summer.

Norway is a northern country, stretching from the sixtieth parallel all the way above the Arctic Circle, where it is the Land of the Midnight Sun. After a long, dark winter, the longer days of summer are a welcome cause for celebration.

* * *

Every year at camp, the "Troll Pack", a select group of senior campers, stole the cutlery. The "trolls" left a message, in rhyme, that they would be appeased and the cutlery returned if the cooks left out a bowl of *Romegrot* for them. Therefore, we had no knives or forks at breakfast or lunch to give time for the preparation of *Romegrot*. The cook knew enough to serve a meal requiring only a spoon. I wonder…how did she know?

---

9   Email from Philip Ramstad

Romegrot was made by adding flour to cream, simmered over a low heat until attaining porridge-like consistency. The secret was in diligently stirring and stirring. When making the larger, harder-to-handle amount for the final camp day celebration, some men proudly took that job. Wielding the large wooden paddle with a gallon or so of cream was heavy work. As it neared completion, yellow butterfat rose to the top of the creamy-white mixture. Drained off and served from a pitcher, the drawn butter was an accent to the dessert, after topping it with brown sugar and cinnamon.

More Norwegian foods:

I was more familiar with *Romegrot's* close relative, a rice porridge, or *Risengrot,* made with one-third of a cup of rice cooked in four cups of milk, in a double-boiler or in a casserole in a low oven, for two or three hours till it was thick and creamy. It, too, was soft and delicious, served with brown sugar and cinnamon, though not as rich as its counterpart.

Flatbrod is literally flat bread, a traditional Norwegian unleavened bread made for centuries with barley flour. Since the crisp, dry bread had excellent keeping qualities, emigrants packed flatbread to keep them on their long ocean voyage.

Blotkake (Cream Cake) is a sponge type cake decorated with whipped cream and fruit, made for special occasions. At camp, it was made to represent a Norwegian flag, with a red strawberry background and an extra piping of whipping cream to outline the slightly off-centered dark blue (berry) cross.

Smørbrød (Norwegian open-face sandwiches) are similar to their Swedish and Danish counterparts. The word literally means "buttered bread", but it goes far beyond that. The bread base must be thinly-sliced firm European style bread—no Wonder Bread allowed!

Each sandwich is a work of art with at least three components. The base may be lettuce, topped with meat, cheese, fish, or eggs completely covering the bread. Then a variety of salad-type accents are arranged artistically to complete the picture. This is not a North American type of sandwich to eat held in your hands. Eat these beauties with a knife and fork.

Kranskake (Crown Cake) is another specialty for occasions like weddings. Ground almonds are the main ingredient. Special ring pans in which each ring gets progressively smaller are used to bake the rolled strips of dough. Then, baked rings are stacked and fastened together with icing, largest to smallest. Then the "crown" is drizzled with white icing garlands and decorated with small paper Norwegian flags. For serving, it is broken apart and the pieces are eaten.

A Norwegian map and sampler shown on the next page, we did in afternoon craft session. It gave me an overview of the various Norwegian needlecrafts. I gave up on my efforts at *rosemaling,* but treasured the gifts I got from Harry. Each year, Harry showed his appreciation for the work that my husband and I did as cooks by giving us a special memento representing the wide variety of artistic Norwegian crafts he was skilled at, ranging from chip carving, scrimshaw, rosemaling to bone carving.

Rosemaling is the name of a decorative folk art,—translated as "flower painting"—that originated in the rural valleys of Norway. It features artistically-stylized floral designs, flowing lines, and subtle earthy colours. Rosemaling decorates furniture, walls, ceilings, and small wooden items. Different styles exist, each named for the region where they developed. Norwegian chip carving uses similar designs in a three-dimensional art done on wood.

***

Folk dancing was a delight to see and hear, for the dances told stories in words, music, and movements. The young students learned the words to *Per Spelmann*, the story of a musician who trades his only cow to get back his good old violin. Per plays that instrument until the fiddle laughs, the boys dance, and the girls cry!

Since there were enough red vests—along with navy breeches for the boys and skirts for the girls—the lilting melody performed as a round dance created an idyllic scene on the grassy lakeshore. The sight transported us to Norway, at least in our imagination.

In 1984 the camp was at Sylvan Lake and my son, Will, (centre) took part in the dancing

Elaine Melby Ayre

FROM TOP TO BOTTOM:

ABOVE THE ARCTIC CIRCLE,
THE REINDEER REPRESENTS
THE LAPLANDERS,

THE WOVEN SUN REPRE-
SENTS "THE LAND OF
THE MIDNIGHT SUN",

PETIT POINT BUILDING- THE
NIDAROS CATHEDRAL WHERE
ST. OLAF, PATRON SAINT
OF NORWAY IS BURIED,

THE NORWEGIAN FLAG
DONE IN STRAIGHT STITCH
- CAPITAL CITY, OSLO,

CROSS STITCHED DANCE
PAIR - BERGEN FOLK FESTI-
VAL HELD EACH SUMMER,

CIRCLE WITH CUTWORK
HARDANGER EMBROIDERY
- HARDANGER FJORD

***

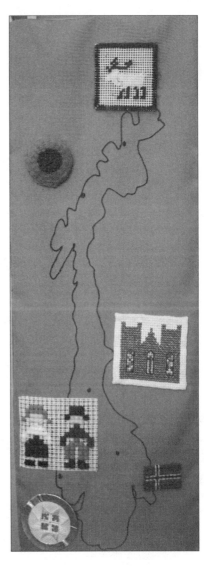

Inevitably, conversations amongst campers led to the following questions: What do you know about your roots in Norway? What region did
they come from? When did they leave? What were their emigration and
immigration experiences? Where did they come to?

Researching the story of Princess's families for this scrapbook encouraged me to find the answers.

Part Three

THE EMIGRANTS

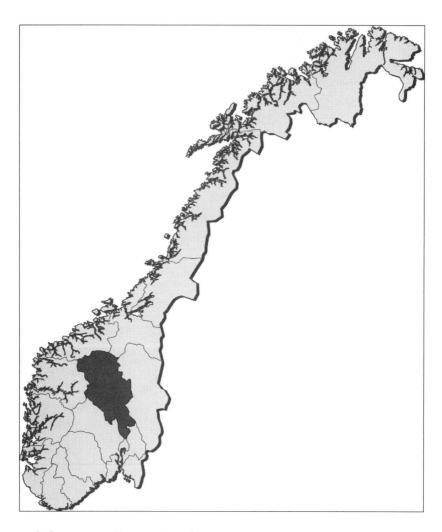

©Canstock Photo Inc./Schwabenblitz. Map of Norway,
with Oppland region highlighted. If you look at the
bottom of the Oppland map as a profile of a person,
the large nose is Ostre Toten. Vestre Toten is up from
the bottom of the nose, straight north of Oslo

Elaine Melby Ayre

Chapter Six

CHECKING OUT THOSE ROOTS

Gamle Norge-Old Norway

Those deeply-buried roots took many twists and turns. Princess's scrapbook became the perfect place to record stories of people from another time and place.

***

Learning about my roots started on a rough, hand-drawn family tree my mother created for me when I was quite young. Seeing that strange name, Maria Kristiansdatter Blaavarp, marked the beginning interest in my family tree. Maria was my great grandmother, my mother's grandmother.

JOHAN AND MARIA GRONVOLD'S 50ᵀᴴ WEDDING ANNIVERSARY

From L-R starting at the back row: Adolph , Helen and Henry, holding Martha, their daughter, Irene standing in between, Mathilda and Jens Gronvold, holding Raymond, Edith, Myrtle, Dina, John Hansen, holding Johnny, and older boys, Alvin and Walter Gronvold, Bernhard and Clarence Hansen, Seated in front of Johan and Maria Gronvold: Clara and Anna Hansen, Evelyn and Marian Gronvold.

ELAINE MELBY AYRE

Several pictures from mother's photo album show her, an old woman, clothed in dark colours, wearing a close-fitting bonnet and a long white apron, the typical traditional fashion for older women in Norway. My mother wrote that her grandmother wore printed shirtwaist tops but in all the pictures I found she is wearing what looks like a man's dark sweater with a shawl collar. Maria was seated front and centre, next to her husband, Johan Gronvold, and surrounded by her family. The occasion was the celebration of their golden wedding anniversary which should have been May 1926 but a date stamped on the back by the photo developer indicates this event took place in 1925 (likely because 1926 was the year my grandfather, JB Hansen went back to Norway).

Once I thought her strange and old-fashioned. Bit by bit, as I uncovered fragments of her story, I gained appreciation for her lifetime experience—and when I recognized it had to have been Maria who selected the doll, my connection to her became even stronger.

***

Piecing records gave me an opportunity to revisit Maria's story in her pre-America days in Norway. Fortunately, most census and church records from Norway are complete. Finding distant cousins who had already done some of this investigation and were willing to share helped my quest immensely.

Almost 100% of Norway's population was part of the State-organized Lutheran Church. This allows searchers to more easily find and follow their ancestors' important life events, starting with their baptism. Law required babies born in rural areas be baptized within eight days of birth, versus four days in cities. In Maria's case, she and her twin sister, Pauline, were born January 17, 1847 and their baptism recorded January 25, 1847. Performing the christening ceremony so soon was important, for the infant mortality in that time was so high. The sacrament assured parents their child was a member of God's family and their name was in the Lamb's Book of Life. In Maria's family alone, three siblings never made it to their first birthday.

Confirmation was a rite of passage that signified reaching adult status and achieving full membership in the church; this took place after a period of studying Luther's Small Catechism to learn the basics of the faith when the young person was about fourteen to fifteen years of age. It was a serious matter, for that Confirmation certificate was a prerequisite for getting married in the church. Beyond those records, there were marriage and death records, even smallpox vaccination records!

**

To learn about Maria's roots, I analyzed the genealogical form for her name and address: *Maria Kristiansdtr. Blaavarp, Vestre Toten, Oppland, Norway.*

Maria was her given or baptismal name. Naming in Norway followed a strict pattern. Her oldest brother, Ole, named for his father's father, then her sister, Bertha, for her father's mother. The next, Pauline, was named for her mother's father, Paul, but the name was made feminine by adding 'ine' (pronounced *eenuh*, emphasis on the *ee*). Her grandfather Paul's stepmother, Mari (to rhyme with *car ee*) was Maria's namesake. When looking at the names of any generation, count on the fact that those names alternated from one generation to the next.

Kristiansdtr. was Maria's patronymic name. The system of naming after the father continued in Scandinavian countries until the end of the 1800s. Maria was the daughter (*datter*) of Kristian, most often abbreviated '*dtr.*' Her brothers were Kristians. or Kristiansen, meaning *son of Kristian*. Many patronymic names remain today as surnames, dating back to some now-unknown great-great-great-great grandfather. Patronymic names occur among other countries in other forms. Two examples are *MacDonald* or *O'Shea*.

Blaavarp was the *Gaard* (farm name): All farms had a name, commonly used as an identifying part of a person's name, as a surname. A person who had lived in several places might add them to the list. Once the patronymic naming system discontinued, farm names became the source of Norwegian surnames.

ELAINE MELBY AYRE

BLAAVARP FARM FROM THE ROAD. PHOTO BY LARRY HANSEN

BLAAVARP HOME[10]

---

10   Photoshopped image by Marlene Atkinson from photocopied picture I received
      from Loyd Erion, a descendant from Maria's sister, Bertha and Ole Espe's family.
      Carving around the doorway and on the upper balcony appear to be an ornate

I found *Blaavarp* on Google Earth, about a half a kilometer from a town called Eina, on the north end of Lake Eina leading to a river of the same name. (Eina was also the name of the parish—or *sogn,* significant, for that is how family records, as described earlier, were organized). Maria's father ran a farm and limekiln at Blaavarp. Lime was used to make cement and mortar.

Vestre Toten was the *Kommune* (municipality) in the southeastern part of the Oppland district, almost straight north of Oslo. When Maria lived there, Oslo went by its old name, Kristiania.

Oppland was the *fylke* (district), the only one out of eighteen of Norway's regions that did not touch the sea or their eastern neighbor, Sweden.

This long narrow country of *Norway* extends from the sixtieth parallel all the way past the Arctic Circle. Its jagged western coast, where mountains meet the fjords, hugs the edge of the Baltic Peninsula.

Understanding how administrative districts and municipalities work in Norway helped me learn about my Norwegian ancestors; remember, similar organizational terms exist for other countries.

***

Now, meet Maria's large four-generation family as they appeared in the 1865 census:[11]

The first individual listed is Maria's father, Kristian Olson, the head of the household, farmer and owner. He was fifty years old; married (designated by the abbreviation 'g' for *gift*) and was born in Vestre Toten. The farm's 'production' listed three horses, ten cows, ten sheep, and two pigs. The grain crops, measured in units called *tonder,* or barrels (equal to 139 liters or 3.95 US bushels), were four of barley, five mixed grain, three quarter unit of peas, and twelve and a half of potatoes. Contrasted to the majority of people on the land in Norway who were tenant farmers

---

form of Norwegian chip carving mentioned in Chapter Five. A flag pole on the left front side of the front door was taken out of the picture.

11   http://digitalarkivet.uib.no/cgiwin/WebCens.exe?slag=visbase&sidenr=3&filnamn=f60529&gardpostnr=1346&personpostnr=7474&merk=7474#ovre

or *husman,* Maria's father's farm appears to be relatively well off. Kristian was the third generation of his family to run this farm.

His wife, Ragnhild Paulsdtr., born in the traditional district, Hadeland, the area now called Gran, was forty-nine years old. Her father was Paul, so she is Paulsdatter (and since Paul and Ole were brothers Ragnhild and Kristian were cousins, a common occurrence in remote areas).

Kristian's daughters were: Maria's twin sister, Pauline, age nineteen, listed as unmarried, as well as Karine, age seventeen, and Severine, age sixteen.

Kristian's sons were Hans, age thirteen, Anton, age ten, and Laurits, age five. As Laurits' birthdate was November 1861, he should be three, coming four at an 1865 census.

Others found their family members' ages off by a year, the most likely explanation was that since the census order was given for December 31, 1865- January1, 1866, the actual census taking began after January 6, 1866.[12] Pauline had a two-year-old son named Ole K (for his great-grandfather, Ole, and grandfather, Kristian) Johannessen. Though Pauline was not married, her child had the father's name, Johannes (the father was from another district).

Also living with them was Kristian's father and the children's *bestefar* (grandfather), a widower, Ole Neilsen, eighty-three years old. His wife, Berte Kristiansdtr, had died in 1861.

The last person listed was a thirty-year-old hired man, Ole Olsen. Though his surname is the same as Kristian, it is hard to say if he has a connection to the family.

Maria was away working as a servant or housekeeper for a more well-to-do family. Someday, I hope to find her listed as a servant in someone's home.

The two oldest from this family had emigrated in 1861—Ole, born in 1838, and Bertha, born in 1842. I wondered if Ole was running away from his obligations, for he left behind two girlfriends and three illegitimate daughters.

---

12   http://www.rhd.uit.no/nhdc/census.html#BM1865 documenting the 1865 census

In the few short months Ole had been in America, he travelled to Iowa County in southwestern Wisconsin where he signed up for the Civil War effort with Company "F" of the famed Scandinavian Regiment-the Fifteenth Wisconsin Volunteer Infantry. Valdres Company was another name given to his regiment, since most of its members came from Valdres, a traditional central area of old Norway. The family now mourned his loss, for five months after joining, he died from disease in May of 1862 at Island No.10 in the Mississippi River about 10 miles upstream from Madrid City, MO.

Bertha married Ole O Espe within a year or two after emigrating, and now lived in Lee County in north central Illinois. At this time, she had two young sons, Kristian and Julius.

***

Two pictures, shown on the next page, exist from this time period. The top one is of Maria's mother, Ragnhild. It was common that a portrait of a family member left behind in Norway came along in their emigrant trunks. I found it strange there would be a picture of Ole when there were none of any other family members.

Looking at the family background gave me a possible answer to the question, "Why would the family allow their youngest son, Laurits, to emigrate with his two older sisters in 1869?"

He was only seven—the baby of the family—although there was now his nephew, three years younger, living in the household. What was their thinking?

The story of the brothers, Ole and Paul, their two grandfathers revealed possible answers. When I looked at Ole and Paul's family of origin, their mother died in 1799, leaving three older sisters, Ole, eleven, Paul, eight, and a five-year-old brother. When their mother's sister, Mari, and her husband, Even, came for the funeral, they took Paul to live with them at their farm.

Skari, in Hadeland, was likely a good day's journey away. In the 1801 census, Even and Mari were fifty-four years of age, and their nephew, Paul (spelled Povel here), age ten, was living with them. Since they had no children, they offered to raise Paul. This was an advantage for Paul, for only his older brother, Ole, had the right to inherit Blaavarp. Eight years after his name appeared in this census, Paul was married and eventually took over the Skari farm, where he died in 1853 at sixty-three years of age. That was how the brothers, Ole and Paul, became separated.

Paul and his wife, Helene, had four daughters. Three sons died very young. Three daughters married in that area. Two of them, Mari and Martha, became part of this emigration story, the first from this family group to leave Norway. Daughter, Ragnhild took a shine to her cousin, Kristian, who lived in the region to the north, and they were married. Kristian and Ragnhild were Maria's parents.

Now since Grandfather Paul had moved away from his parental home to another district for an aunt and uncle to bring up, it was not so strange that seventy years later, Laurits left his. His parents, at fifty-three and fifty-two years of age, likely considered themselves old, and thought opportunities would be better for him in America.

Besides those factors, there was another prospect I couldn't prove, yet it seemed likely. An online history of a Newquist family from Sweden, whose ancestors came to America the same time Maria did, said starvation was their ancestor's main reason for emigrating. Crops had failed for several years in the latter years of the 1860s. Several other cousins connected to my story repeated that explanation, for they had ancestors on the other side of their family who emigrated then, all because of starvation.

But did the fact, that only one of Kristian and Ragnhild's nine surviving children remained in Norway, have anything to do with a supposed black mark on the family?

After my mother visited Maria's home area in Norway in the early 1970s, her brief comment was, "Sometimes when you go looking, you find out more than you want to know."

What this story was, she never could or would tell me. I developed far-fetched theories. Eventually, when I found the actual story, none of my theories were even close.

When my distant cousin, Garth, shared his comprehensive family tree, going back to Maria's father, Kristian Olsen and further, there it was in black and white. Though Maria's twin sister, Pauline had an illegitimate son, as we saw in the census, a child born out of wedlock wasn't uncommon. Fines and having to offer public confession in the church had once been the response. Authorities checked that the father provided child support which might explain, but not excuse, the next event.

The next entry was this revelation:

"Male child, born and died in 1867. Lars denied paternity, and Pauline took the baby's life during birth."

The issue was neonaticide (infanticide carried out at birth). What reaction was there in this community back then, if, over a hundred years later, it was still related as a black mark? Might this have been a reason for the emigration of most in the family?

I saw Pauline, the older of the twins, as the "boy crazy type" while Maria, steady and hardworking, saved, bit by bit, towards her goal of emigrating.

***

The winds of change were moving across Norway—and all of Europe, for that matter. The population was increasing at a high rate, and the half of the population that made their living by farming struggled away on small plots of land. I remembered discovering in other family history research I had done on my Melby family side, about how that farm was eventually divided up to twenty times. Increasingly smaller farms meant making a decent living less possible.

> "Though government officials and the clergy tried to discourage leaving the homeland ….to the hard-working farmer struggling to keep above poverty on a small plot of land in Norway, the vision of 160 acres of free land was the final compelling argument."[13]

By the time the massive migrations of the nineteenth century slowed down, Norway was second only to Ireland in the proportion of its population that had emigrated.[14]

What was the emigrant experience like for my ancestors in the 1800s? It had always been something I'd been curious about. It wasn't an event that happened over a day or two, like today; emigrating took weeks or months, as we will see.

---

13   Gulbrand Loken *From Fjord to Frontier- A history of the Norwegians in Canada* McClelland and Stewart Ltd 1980 264 pages p30

14   Gulbrand Loken *From Fjord to Frontier- A history of the Norwegians in Canada* McClelland and Stewart Ltd 1980 264 pages p30

Chapter Seven

EXODUS I

In the winter of 1848-49 in a district north of Oslo, Norway, known as Hadeland, Hans "…sat reading of a fabled spot in the United States called Iowa, where new land was to be offered for sale at ridiculously low prices."

Hans was described as "…a strapping giant of a man, with great physical strength, with a shock of coal black hair, and a reputation of being the local *kjaempe* or champion (every locality in Norway in those days had theirs)."

Maria's second cousin, Clarence Petersen, wrote an article titled "The Saga of the House of Lovbroden," published in the Decorah Public Opinion, January 28, 1942. This addition to the scrapbook highlighted her Aunt Martha and Uncle Hans's earlier emigration/immigration experience.

Inspired by his childhood memories from the 1880s; Clarence remembered when he was eight years of age how he had enjoyed a hearty Sunday dinner at his grandfather's home. Afterwards, the menfolk lay down on the shaded green lawn to rest and visit:

"When cigars and pipes were going well, my grandfather would usually remove his Sunday shoes, as well as his stockings… Then, perfectly at ease, he would start reminiscing about the pioneer days, and we boys would be all ears, drinking in every word…"[15]

***

Now, what was Hans reading? Advertisements in Norwegian newspapers told of land for sale, but was not yet reporting about homesteading land. The United States Homesteading Act didn't come into effect until 1862, (and the Canadian Dominion Lands Act not until 1872). It might have been reports from Cleng Peerson, who had explored and examined the new land to find what it had to offer. Whether it was a personal letter, a book or a newspaper article, it convinced Hans to take the next step.

The Father of Norwegian-American Immigration

In 1825, Cleng Peerson led a group of fifty-two Norwegian Quakers on the sloop, *Restauration* seeking relief from an intolerant state church. Their October 9, 1825 arrival at New York is considered an historic landmark for Norwegians. Four years earlier, this group sponsored Cleng to search out a suitable place for them in the New World. The group experienced difficult times in the place he found in Orleans County in upper New York State, yet Cleng believed America had better things to offer.

In 1833, he set out on foot, going first to Chicago, and then to Milwaukee. When he found out that north of there was only woods, and more woods,

---

15   Clarence Petersen "The Saga of the House of Lovbroden" *Decorah Public Opinion* January 28, 1942. Article shared with me by Philip Ramstad and used by permission of the *Decorah Public Opinion* editor.

he went south. He literally found the spot of his dreams in LaSalle County, in northern Illinois. Returning to the group in New York, he convinced them to move to the area that became the Fox River Settlement.

Word got back to Norway about low-cost, fertile land, ready for the plow. When all suitable land was taken, Cleng continued searching through Missouri and southeastern Iowa for more areas in which to settle. During this period, he made seven trips back to Norway. Finally, in 1854, he made Texas his home.

By the 1840s, other writers urged Norwegian peasants to seek a better future in America:

Ole Rynning had a thirty-nine-page book, titled *True Account of America*, published in 1837.

Nattestad wrote a similar book in 1838 after returning from a trip to America.

Reiersen, editor of the Norwegian newspaper *Kristiansandsposten*, visited Fox River in 1843, reported on Cleng Peerson's findings, and published a book called *Pathfinder for Norwegian Emigrants to the North American States and Texas*. Texas at that time was not yet part of the United States.[16]

Now Hadeland, where Hans and Marthe lived, was one of the best farming districts in all of Norway. Though the previous year's potato,

16   History of the Norwegian Settlements (Norske Settlementers Historie and the 1930 Den Siste Folkevandring Sagastubber fra Nybyggerlivet in Amerika by Hjalmer Rued Holand) Translated by Malcolm Rosholt and Helmer M. Blegen Published by Astri My Astri Publishing, Waukon, Iowa, 2006 Chapter 3 tells about Cleng Peerson. Used by permission of the publisher

barley, and hay crops had been good, Hans felt an urge to travel to this land of opportunity with his wife and two young daughters. After they decided, their preparation started with the purchase of two large home-made white pine chests from a local cabinetmaker.

> "These chests were large …, with roomy, rounded tops, and each equipped with a homemade lock and massive iron key, some three inches in length. Chests were painted in rich red, with address written in freehand style in white paint – Hans Lovbroten, Lansing, Iowa, U.S."[17]

A transatlantic trip by sailing ship required careful preparation. Into the two chests went cherished articles from their home in Norway: wooden cups and spoons, clothing, yards upon yards of the coarse woolen homespun cloth, known as *wadmal,* and Hans's Bible.

Since their meals were not included, they also had to stock up with food. The average time for the crossing was fifty-three days; their voyage on the sailing ship *Vesta* took fifty-eight days from Christiania (now Oslo) to New York City. Ship companies' lists suggested they bring enough for a ten-week trip, including items such as large blocks of homemade cheeses, quantities of bread, and dried beef or mutton for their meals, along with utensils for cooking and preparing their coffee and tea. Their water pail had to be large enough to hold their allotted three quarts per person per day. This would be their allotment for drinking as well as washing.[18]

---

17 Clarence Petersen "The Saga of the House of Lovbroden" Decorah Public Opinion January 28, 1942. Used with permission.

18 http://www.norwayheritage.com/provisions.htm

ELAINE MELBY AYRE

"THE ROLL CALL AT SEA"[19]

A drawing from this period "Exhibits a review of the passengers, by the officers, to ascertain their sanitary condition, and to see if they have complied with the regulations. They pass up the starboard gangway to the upper deck, and return to the main deck by the port side. All the internal economy of an emigrant ship is based on rigid system and under the control of the law"

***

This was a large family group. They were joined by Martha's sister, Mari, her husband Hans, and six children. Their eldest son, Juel, had emigrated the year earlier. What a trip this must have been for Mari! Sometime during that voyage she gave birth to a girl, Oline Fredrikka Vesta. It was customary for babies born on the transatlantic voyage to

---

19   From *Ballou's Pictorial Drawing-Room Companion*, Not dated, Collection of Maggie Land Blanck, Used with permission

be named for the captain, the ship, or the ocean. In this case, it was for the ship. This was a May 1849 sailing, and Mari's youngest child, Hans (born 25 Sept 1848), was only a little over seven months old as the trip began. I 'guesstimated' difficulties encountered on those fifty-eight days likely led to this child's premature birth. This child's name never appeared in later censuses. An epidemic of cholera swept the Norwegian immigrant community that winter, and likely claimed the life of this young baby. The rest of the family survived this first extreme test.

***

"After…weeks of arduous travel the emigrant ship finally docked…many more days of travel lay ahead of the Norwegian party before they arrived…"

In the days before transcontinental train travel, the trip Maria's relatives underwent was much like this description from *History of the Norwegian Settlements* by Holand:

"Very few of the immigrants had any concept of the vastness of length and breadth of America. When they reached New York harbor, many thought they were near their destination. Had they known they still had several weeks of less-than-desirable living conditions ahead before they reached the West, no doubt many of them would have completely despaired.

For after New York, there still remained the steamship ride up to Albany on the Hudson River, and from there a (360-mile-long) journey by canal boat west to Buffalo on the Erie Canal, where the traveler had to cross the Great Lakes before reaching Milwaukee or Chicago…"[20]

---

20   History of the Norwegian Settlements (Norske Settlementers Historie and
      the 1930 Den Siste Folkevandring Sagastubber fra Nybyggerlivet in Amerika
      by Hjalmer Rued Holand) Translated by Malcolm Rosholt and Helmer M.
      Blegen, Astri My Astri Publishing, Waukon, Iowa, 2006 page 27 Used by
      permission

Canal boats were barges with a deck pulled along by one or two mules. The speed was up to three miles per hour. Unnecessary delays aside, a trip from Albany to Buffalo took about twelve days.

> "Even if the accommodations on board had not been so miserable, it was still not possible to sleep. The entire trip was one continuous and maddening bustle to negotiate the many canal locks, of which there were no fewer than eighty-three. Added to this was the commotion of discharging cargo at frequent stops, the banging together with other boats, the coarse language heard between the barge captains, and the uproar that followed when the barge now and then became stranded on a sandbar." [21]

***

Muskego, twenty miles south of Milwaukee, Wisconsin, was one of the first places Norwegians settled. Muskego looked good in the summer, but fall rains brought out swamp-like conditions, leading to dreaded outbreaks of cholera and malaria. In a short time, many moved on to more attractive locations. Yet because of its location on the western shore of Lake Michigan at the end of the inland trip via the Great Lakes, Muskego had the reputation as the original Norwegian settlement, for the first church and the first Norwegian newspaper began there.

These early families first went to Yorkville Prairie, a settlement south of Muskego. Both of these families were fortunate to share the hospitality of two brothers during that first winter. Hans and Martha were put up with Nils Johnsen, and Mari and Hans with Gjermund Johnsen families. The Johnsens were not related to them nor even from the same district – were they just helping out their fellow countrymen?

***

---

21   As footnote 20 page 28,29

A book listing all the individuals and families leaving Maria's district, transcribed to the web as *The Toten Emigrant Project*, told about the 1853 rush of emigrants that included the next family members.[22]

> "In the late 1840s, with the best areas of land in Wisconsin occupied, settlers sought new lands west of the Mississippi. They were particularly interested in areas of the existing Counties of Fillmore and Houston in southeast Minnesota, and Allamakee and Winneshiek in northeast Iowa for here were forests, water and fertile soil.

> "The Norwegians came to Allamakee, and to Winneshiek, the neighbouring county on the west. They came in multitudes, and Winneshiek soon became the county in Iowa where Norwegians were the largest group. Glenwood Township (on the western edge of Allamakee County) became the first major settlement of people from Toten during the 1850s [including Hans and Martha Lovbraaten]. In Toten and anywhere in Eastern Norway, there was great interest in America. Elias Stangeland had traveled around lecturing about the country in the winter of 1852-53. People attended in great numbers to hear about America and decided that they would take off next spring. The party was very large—the largest to have emigrated from the Vestre Toten at one time [and included Maria's paternal aunt, Anne Mathea and her husband, Neils and their two young children, Ole and Bertha]. They left Oslo on 28th April 1853 on the sailing ship <u>Deodata</u> under the command of Captain Skrøder, and landed in Quebec, Canada, seven weeks later."[23]

---

22   https://sites.google.com/site/totenemigrant/Toten-emigrant-1846/1851-1855
      (*Translated from Norwegian*)

23   Ingrid Semmingsen *Veien mot vest 1825-1865* Aschehoug 1942 Used with
      permission of the publisher. This quote was found on the *Toten Emigrant*

Sailing ships, like the one Anne Mathea and Neils came on, were called Barks. Trips on sailing ships could take up to three months, depending on the whims of winds and weather. Now many immigrant ships came to Quebec City. It was a shorter route, direct from Norway. The ships returned to Norway with cargo in the holds that accommodated passengers on their westbound trip to the New World, making cheap, affordable fares possible. This route became a factor in the decreased need for the Erie Canal in transporting immigrants to the Midwest.

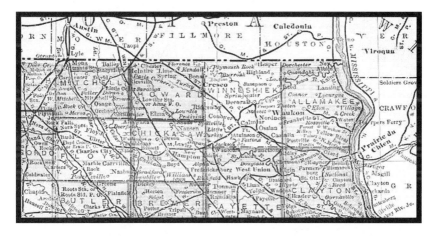

MAP OF NORTHEAST IOWA AND SOUTHEAST MINNESOTA SHOWING COUNTIES WHERE FAMILY MEMBERS LIVED
(PORTION FROM CANSTOCK PHOTO 5912280, USED WITH PERMISSION)

Project. (Translated from Norwegian)

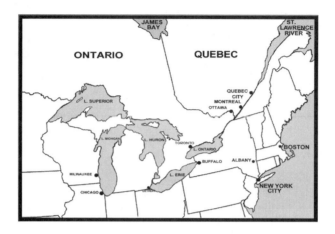

TRACE THE ROUTES TO THE MIDWEST[24]

Now, those travellers faced three more weeks travelling by a variety of methods: steamer down the St Lawrence through to Lake Ontario, some by walking (where they undoubtedly got a glimpse of Niagara Falls), to Lake Erie, then by rail from Detroit to Chicago, and by steamer to the western shore of Lake Michigan. Another route was by steamer to Toronto, train to Collingwood, and by steamer across Lake Huron and Lake Michigan to Green Bay, Milwaukee, and Chicago.

***

I was most interested in the story of Maria's trip, but once I learned about them, I recognized her trip happened against the background of seventeen relatives who came ahead of her.

First to come, in 1848, was her adventurous seventeen-year-old cousin, Juel Hansen Skari. Maria was only a year old.

In 1849, Juel's parents, Aunt Mari, her husband Hans, and their other six children emigrated—along with her aunt Martha and husband Hans Pedersen Lovbraaten and their two young daughters. Therefore, by the time Maria was old enough to comprehend, she heard about her

---

24   This image is a portion of a North American map ©CanstockInc,/ /JonnyCloud. Places marked on the map are approximate, photoshopped byMarlene Atkinsen

ELAINE MELBY AYRE

mother's sisters and her cousins in America, including as many that were American-born.

In 1853, Maria's sixth year, the family said farewell to family that lived in the same area—their father's sister, Anne Mathea, her husband, Neils Voldeng and two young children, Ole and Bertha.

When Maria was fourteen in 1861, her oldest brother and sister emigrated, though not at the same time. However, by 1862, her brother, Ole (who had joined the Fifteenth Wisconsin Regiment's Civil War effort), had died of disease.

A most difficult farewell had to be when Maria's oldest sister Bertha received her certificate (called an *Attest*) on 22 Apr 1861. This document gave Bertha permission from the authorities to leave Norway. She sailed away on the bark *Garibaldi* on 3 May 1861 and landed in Quebec 20 June 1961. The American Civil War was into its third month by the time Bertha reached Lake Michigan's western shore. (Numbers of emigrants almost ceased then and new immigrants dealt with the turmoil in their new country.)

With other family leading the exodus and emigration firmly planted in her mind, Maria determined to join them soon. Meanwhile, she worked away from home as a servant or housekeeper for a more well-to-do family as this was the only type of employment available to a woman in that time and place.

Wages were extremely low, as explained, years later, by Maria's son:

> "In Norway, a girl's wages were $7.00 a year; of course
> she got everything else including clothing, shoes, etc.
> No wonder they came to America."[25]

Nonetheless, Maria persevered until she had enough to pay the fare and the right opportunity presented itself.

---

25   Jens Gronvold's unpublished informal story about his mother, Maria and father, Johan from family memorabilia, written about 1960

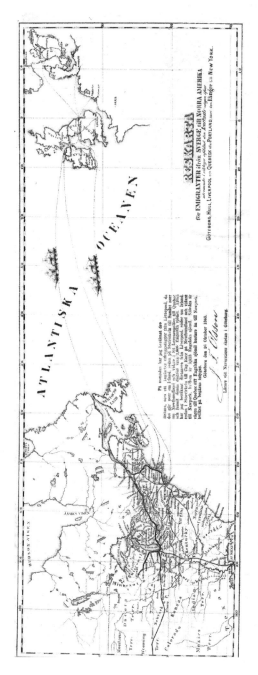

Routes 1869- from an old booklet- A map issued by the Allan Line general agent in Sweden 1869. It shows different routes for emigrants wishing to immigrate to Canada and the United States. Text is in Swedish.

www.norwayheritage.com

Courtesy of the Norway Heritage Collection - www.norwayheritage.com. Source: www.heritage-ships.com

ELAINE MELBY AYRE

Chapter Eight

EXODUS II

The long-awaited day arrived. Maria was able to leave Norway to join her family in America. Times had changed. Now steamships and the completion of the American transcontinental railway would give Maria an improved travel experience.

26

26   http://www.maggieblanck.com/Immigration.html Picture is titled
       "Land Farewell" From the Collection of Maggie Land Blanck Used with

In spite of the excitement, leaving their family and country behind filled them with sadness this picture expressed. I imagined Maria with Laurits, her seven-year-old brother, watching their last sight of Norway slip below the horizon.

Kan du glemme, Gamle Norge[27]

How can you forget old Norway,
Land of rock and narrow fjords
Where the mountains are like castles
And stand like sentinels on guard.

How can you forget old Norway,
Land of everlasting fame.
Can you ever find another
With so glorious a name?

How can you forget old Norway
And its narrow fjords so grand,
In and out between the mountains,
Tis my home , my native land

Maria, with her sister, Karine, and youngest brother, Laurits, are listed as entries 1869/398, 399, and 400 on *The Toten Emigrant Project.*[28] They and others sailed away, 11 May 1869 on the ship <u>Skandinavia</u>, on the first leg of what had now become a two-part trip to America.

***

permission

27 The translation of this song was included with an MP3 of
The Radio Stars performing it at the Minot, North Dakota's
Hostfest, October 2013 and shared in an email from Hermod
Monsen

28 All emigrants that left Toten kommune of the Oppland area of Norway
were recorded in a book titled **Utvandringen til Amerika fra Totenbygdene
1846-1966.**

Answers to my questions about Maria's emigrant experiences were found on the Norway Heritage website.

Den korteste og meest directe Vei
fra
Norge og Sverige
til
Amerika
er med

ANKER LINIENS NORDSØ DAMPSKIBE

SCOTIA & SCANDINAVIA,
som seile hver Uge fra
Christiania og Christianssand
ogsaa fra
Gothenborg
til
New-York
via Edinborg & Glasgow
i Forbindelse med deres atlantiske Dampskibsflaade.
Man henvende sig til Eierne
Henderson Brothers,
Hjørnet af Prindsens og Skippergaden,
Christiania,

THE "TRAVEL BROCHURE" FOR MARIA'S TRIP[29]

29   Courtesy of the Norway Heritage Collection- www.norwayheritage.com
       Source: www.heritage-ships.com

"Henderson Brothers based in Christiania, now known as Oslo, were the general agents for the Anchor Line. The sailings were every Tuesday afternoon at five o'clock, calling at Christiansand (around on Norway's southern coast) on Wednesday morning at ten. The ships sailed for Edinburgh, Scotland. From there they connected by train with Glasgow. The Anchor line's transatlantic steamships left out of Glasgow for New York twice a week. For steerage accommodation from Christiania to New York, the fee was 33 *Speciedaler* (about $39), 2nd class accommodation was 42 Spd. (about $49), and 1st class was between 75 and 85 Spd."[30]

Maria, like most emigrants, paid for steerage accommodations. *Speciedaler* (abbreviated *Spd*) was an old monetary unit, used from Danish times. Later, this became the *Kroner*.

The Scandinavia was a feeder (and smaller) ship for Wilson Line to Leith in Scotland. Leith's docks are the port for Edinburgh. From Leith it was a two-hour, forty-five-mile rail trip to Glasgow where Maria and her sister and young brother boarded a transatlantic steamship. The Leith to Glasgow rail trip was a shortcut, an alternative to going around Scotland by ship. A two-part trip like this was common for most Norwegian emigrants, and also for emigrants from other European countries. European emigrants came to ports on the east coast of northern England or Scotland, and took a train across to sail out from the corresponding western port at Liverpool or Glasgow.

***

---

30   http://www.norwayheritage.com/p_shiplist.asp?co=ancho Used with permission

Finding the name of the ship Maria boarded in Glasgow eluded me until I was directed to a family history blog telling of another family's original emigrants—a young couple, Elias and Kari, who left Norway on the same date and ship my three did. On a partial copy of page seven of the Britannia's passenger list were Elias and Kari's names. So Britannia was the larger ship that completed Maria's transatlantic journey.

I searched for Elias on Ancestry.com and connected with the Britannia manifest (or passenger list), my missing link. Inspecting the pages and finding their names, Maria, Karine and Laurits Christiansdatter, on page eight of Britannia's manifest was a thrill. The record states they were from Sweden, because Norway was still under Swedish rule at this time. The names of Scottish and a few Irish emigrants, who joined them in Glasgow for the balance of the trip to America, filled the remaining seven of fifteen pages.

> Scandinavia[31] was built by C & W Earle in Hull, England, in 1865, four years before the three siblings boarded. Its burden was 615 gross, its dimensions 203.5 feet x 26.1 feet x 16 feet. For comparison, a hockey rink is 200 feet by 85 feet. It was built with two masts, bark rigged, clipper stem, iron construction, single screw, and had a service speed of nine knots. A picture of this ship is on the Anchor line service booklet shown on page 71.

> The ship, Britannia,[32] was larger, its burden being 1,392 gross, with dimensions of 261.5 feet length and a beam of 33.1 feet. It was iron construction with a clipper stem, one funnel, three masts, a single screw and service speed of ten knots. There was accommodation for forty first-class, ninety second-class, and 300 third-class passengers.

31 http://www.norwayheritage.com/p_ship.asp?sh=scada

32 http://www.norwayheritage.com/p_ship.asp?sh=brit0

33

---

33   Courtesy of the Norway Heritage Collection - www.norwayheritage.com
      Source: www.heritage-ships.com From a newspaper advertisement the same
      year Maria traveled.

ELAINE MELBY AYRE

On Maria's trip, twenty years after her aunts, uncles and cousins, a twelve-day ocean journey was typical, as compared to a month or more of travel time. Steamships changed the quality of the ocean passage from potentially deadly to merely uncomfortable.[34] The shorter trip time reduced the threat of epidemics. Another advance was that Maria didn't have to scramble to arrange transportation to the centre of the new continent, as had her earlier relatives. A train ticket to Chicago was included in the price of passage as the advertisement from 1869 indicates.

Besides the shortened travel time, legislation passed in 1869 (the same year Maria travelled) sought to improve the difficult situations emigrants faced. Laws addressed the conditions on the ships that carried folks to the New Land, and made improvements in England/Scotland's facilities where the travelers waited for their train passage to the western side of the British Isles. Legislation also dealt with the issues of deceit and fraud on the part of agents that new emigrants might contend with as they started out and once they set foot in America. The 1869 situation was better, but a sight-seeing or pleasure cruise it was not.

***

The brochure introduced earlier said the menu on board the ship to England was the same as the menu on board the ship to America. Passengers could drink all the water they wanted. Advertisements from the Anchor Line promised passengers would receive the following, during the entire passage from Norway to New York:[35]

---

34   http://www.pgsa.org/Resources/primer.php

35   http://www.norwayheritage.com/by_steamship.htm

**BETWEEN DECKS IN AN EMIGRANT SHIP- FEEDING TIME:
A SKETCH FROM LIFE.** *THE GRAPHIC* **NOV 30, 1873**[36]

36   Commercial usage paid for rights to publish this picture from www.Norway
      Heritage.com

ELAINE MELBY AYRE

". . . so much of the best food, properly prepared, as they could eat, namely:

Breakfast 9 a.m. Tea, coffee or hot chocolate, sugar, bread and butter or biscuits and butter.

Dinner, 1 p.m. Soup, beef or pork with potatoes, with plum pudding on Sundays.

Supper 6 p.m. Tea, coffee or hot chocolate, sugar, bread and butter or biscuits and butter."

Certainly very basic, but an emigrant who traveled with this company described the food like this:

". . . for supper there was…sweet tea without milk in it and dry hard biscuits or Ship's bread, and the same for breakfast. There was butter…so rancid that we could not digest it. For dinner, meat, but there was no taste to the soup or for us Norwegians it had a disgusting taste, and the meat was as salty as herring. One day we had salted fish with a dash of soup, but it was inedible for most of us and it was just to dump our portions into the sea."[37]

Another emigrant journeyed to America with the Guion Line steam-ship Idaho from Liverpool in 1869 had a bigger complaint:

"…You can imagine what an unpleasant journey it was with over 1,100 emigrants crammed together; most of us were treated worse than wild animals. We hardly ate anything at the start of the journey…When we began to understand the situation, and our own provisions were not enough, we had to accept the food that the pigs ate…When we walked on deck, the muck went over our shoes and into the meat container; one should

---

37   http://www.norwayheritage.com/by_steamship.htm From a translation of an 1869 letter sent home to Norway

wash it, but the Irishmen had washed their children's messes and night pots first…"[38]

Had they stashed enough food away, like flatbread and cheese, to augment the meager rations offered by the steamship line? The earlier family travelers, entirely responsible to provide and cook their own food, had to take turns to cook it in a common galley. This must have been a real hardship, especially when other ethnic groups shared the voyage. It was one thing to have to share with a fellow citizen with whom you had a common language, but a different matter when thrust together with strangers speaking a different language and practicing different customs as we can see by the preceding comment.

STEERAGE PASSENGERS[39]

38   http://www.norwayheritage.com/by_steamship.htm

39   *Graphic* March 12, 1870 From the Collection of Maggie Land Blanck.
      Used with permission. http://www.maggieblanck.com/ImmigrationPhotos/

Primitive and *crowded*, *dark* and *damp* described steerage accommodation on board emigrant ships. Entry was via a steep set of stairs, more like a ladder.

Engravings and drawings from this period shows us what it was like.

> "Steerage No. 1 is virtually in the eyes of the vessel, and runs clear across from one side to the other, without a partition. It is lighted entirely by port-holes, under which, fixed to the stringers, are narrow tables with benches before them. The remaining space is filled with iron bunks, row after row, tier upon tier, all running fore and aft in double banks. A thin iron rod is all that separates one sleeper from another. In each bunk are placed "a donkey's breakfast" (a straw mattress), a blanket of the horse variety, a battered tin plate and pannikin, a knife, a fork, and a spoon. This completes the emigrant's "kit," which in former days had to be found by himself.[40]

As for privacy, there was none. Concessions for propriety gave single women accommodation in the bow of the ship, families in the middle, and single men in the stern. It was interesting to note their seven-year-old brother, Laurits listed as female on the manifest; maybe because he stayed with his sisters.

Within their emigrant trunks, they had their own bedding to use on the voyage and in their prospective homes, once they got there. Inevitably, rough and stormy seas meant lockdown for the human cargo in steerage. With the hatch closed and no windows, a passenger's only option was to wait it out in the dark on their bunk. They could not light candles or lanterns because of the danger of fire. Now, think of the individuals who suffered from seasickness. The stench from those that were sick would cause the ones with strong stomachs to be nauseated.

Sept280913.jpg

40   *Steerage Conditions in 1898 - A First-Hand Account* By H. Phelps Whitmarsh, *Century Magazine*, February 1898 as quoted on http://www.maggieblanck.com/ ImmigrationPhotos/Sept280913.jpg used with permission

Emigrant ship conditions were similar, no matter the country of origin. Limited sanitation and stormy seas was the combination that made steerage accommodation dirty and foul-smelling. Primitive toilet facilities shared by large numbers of people added to the unpleasant smells. I hope they brought along their own chamberpot.

***

Difficulties aside, they did make it. Maria, along with her sister, Karine, and their young brother, Laurits, arrived in New York on June 8, 1869, less than a month after departing from Norway. The new world lay before them. They had arrived in the Promised Land—but like the Israelites of old, many obstacles and difficulties remained ahead.

Chapter Nine

THE NEW LAND

"*Er vi der ennå* (Are we there yet)?"

Like any travel-weary child, I imagined seven-and-a-half-year-old Laurits saying this as America's shore loomed that June 8, 1869 morning. Twenty-nine days earlier, they had left Old Norway. Except for the short train trip across Scotland, most of their two-part journey had been at sea.

Filled with excitement—and more than a bit of apprehension at what lay ahead—Laurits and his sisters, Maria and Karine, waited among the passengers crowding the deck of the steamship Britannia.

That morning the captain's instruction had been, "Be ready for inspection," and the Captain's word was law.

Britannia's passengers had undergone inspection before they could officially board in Glasgow. Then, four days into the trip, the ship's doctor checked them for smallpox vaccination.

All vessels coming into New York harbour were subject to quarantine inspection. Britannia's ship doctor presented his report to the health officials when they boarded. Then, as a quick check to see if there were obvious cases of diseases like smallpox, all immigrants paraded past them with their heads uncovered. First and second-class passengers were not subject to inspection. Only then could the ship proceed through the Narrows to the upper bay and anchor not far from New York.[41]

---

41 http://www.maggieblanck.com/Immigration.html

Since the harbour was not deep enough for the larger boats to moor against land, smaller boats, called *lighters*, ferried passengers (and cargo) by turns to the Battery and Castle Gardens in New York. This facility, built early in the 1800s, was an impressive building with spacious grounds where they finally get to try out their rubbery sea legs. Solid land felt strange for a while.

FIRST SIGHT OF NEW YORK BAY - ARRIVAL OF A EUROPEAN STEAMER. - HARPER'S WEEKLY, JUNE 2, 1877[42]

---

42   (First Sight of New York Bay - Arrival of a European Steamer. - Harper's Weekly, June 2, 1877) Credit:Picture Collection , The New York Public Library, Astor, Lenox and Tilden Foundations

© CanStockPhotoInc/stocksnapper Landing
immigrants at Castle Gardens. Harper's
New Monthly Magazine June 1884

THE LABOUR EXCHANGE[43]

43 Library of Congress Prints and Photographs Division
    The Labour Exchange- Emigrants on the Battery in front of Castle Garden, New
    York. Wooden engraving after Stanley Fox, An illustration in Harper's Weekly,
    1868 Aug 15

Battery and Castle Gardens

The Battery's placement at the prow of the island of Manhattan enabled it to serve many roles in New York City's history. Located at the confluence of the Hudson and East Rivers, early Dutch settlers landed here in 1623, and erected the first "battery" of cannons to defend the young city of New Amsterdam.

With the defenses and land enlarged over the years, Castle Clinton was built in anticipation of the War of 1812. A decade later, it became the city's leading cultural center as Castle Garden.

By 1855, successive landfills enlarged the park encompassing Castle Garden. The structure was America's first immigrant receiving center, welcoming 8.5 million people before the establishment of Ellis Island. In an 1896 transformation, the Castle became the New York Aquarium, one of the nation's first public aquariums.

Following near-total demolition in 1941 and a major preservation battle, an Act of Congress in 1946 declared the original fort walls a National Monument. Restored to its fortification appearance by the National Park Service in 1975, the Castle now houses an interpretive display and the ticket office for the ferry to the Statue of Liberty and Ellis Island.[44]

Unfortunately, Castle Garden was not a closed-off area. Hucksters, thieves and ne'er-do-wells had direct access to bewildered immigrants. Ever since the first Norwegian emigrant set foot there, it had been known

---

44   www.thebattery.org/the-battery/history/ used with permission

that they must be wary. Some bought phony tickets for travel to the interior, and some had their much-needed resources robbed. Maria's ticket included travel to Chicago. Though her final destination was Decorah, Iowa, it was an improvement over what earlier emigrants had faced.

The Statue of Liberty was not part of Maria's New York experience, for legendary "Liberty" was not a reality until 1886. In 1890, Ellis Island, which was a closed-off area, became the receiving point for new American immigrants.

I experienced Maria's New York arrival through pictures and articles from magazines and newspapers on Maggie Blanck's excellent website of her family's history in particular, and immigration in general. These illustrations transported me back to 1869 and scrapbooked Maria's arrival.[45]

The Castle Garden's Emigrant Processing Experience

All being ready, Maria and her fellow passengers proceeded in a group up the corridor into the interior of the building where they arranged themselves in order on the seats. Their boxes and baggage had been taken to the luggage warehouses.

A glass dome lit the center of the building. In front of them stood a staff of a dozen men, all occupied in making arrangements to help promote the settlement of the newly-arrived emigrants. Each emigrant—man, woman and child—passed up in turn to the Bureau, and gave to the registrar his or her name and destination as a check upon their ship's Captain's list (manifest), which recorded their name, place of birth, age and occupation. A leading officer with the Bureau of Information mounted a platform

---

45   www.maggieblanck.com used with permission

ELAINE MELBY AYRE

to speak to the assembled emigrants, telling them the following:

Shelter under the roof of the building could be taken, if needed.

The most reliable information regarding the quickest routes to take for railway and steamer tickets in any direction was available.

The Intelligence Department of the Institution kept an employment register and provided advice for obtaining jobs.

There were facilities for corresponding with friends or for changing money at the Bureau of Exchange.

Sick emigrants were to be transferred to a medical facility where they would receive the best of care.

All of these services were provided without charge-(yet how much of that information would the Norwegian emigrants be able to understand?) Maria, Karine and Laurits were among approximately 250,000 immigrants processed in this facility that year of 1869.[46]

***

Processing completed, few people stopped over in New York. Most arrivals made their way to trains or boats and headed west right away. The terminals for the trains heading west, northwest, and south were a ferry trip across the river to Jersey City and Hoboken, New Jersey.

---

46   Adapted from the Newquist Family History website, used with permission

Here, we can take a look at Maria's next experience via Robert Louis Stevenson's emigrant diary.

Deciding to travel to America as an emigrant ten years later, twenty-eight-year-old Stevenson, future author of the novels *Kidnapped* and *Treasure Island*, took advantage of low one-way fares offered by the American railroads. Special "Emigrant Boats" sailed to America's eastern ports; "Emigrant Trains" carried the foreign passengers to their final destinations. His experience became a book from which the website, *EyeWitness to History,* quotes:

"Traveling on an Emigrant Train, 1879".

Stevensen and his fellow emigrants were about to cross on the Hudson River ferry to board the Emigrant Train on a windy, rainy day in New York. He described the rush and confusion:

> "There was a Babel of bewildered men, women, and children. The wretched little booking office, and the baggage room, which was not much larger, were crowded thick with emigrants, and were heavy and rank with the atmosphere of dripping clothes. [Most clothes of the time were made of wool, with its characteristic smell when wet.]

> "I followed the porters into a long shed reaching downhill from West Street to the river. It was dark, the wind blew clean through it from end to end; and here I found a great block of passengers and baggage, hundreds of one and tons of the other. I feel I shall have a difficulty to make myself believed; and certainly, the scene must have been exceptional, for it was too dangerous for daily repetition. It was a tight jam; there was no fair way through the mingled mass of brute and living obstruction. Into the upper skirts of the crowd, porters, infuriated by hurry and overwork, clove their way with shouts.

"The landing at Jersey was done in, a stampede. I had a fixed sense of calamity, and to judge by conduct, the same persuasion was common to us all. A panic selfishness, like that produced by fear, presided over the disorder of our landing. People pushed—and elbowed—and ran, their families following how they could. Children fell, and were picked up to be rewarded by a blow. One child, who had lost her parents, screamed steadily and with increasing shrillness, as though verging towards a fit; an official kept her by him, but no one else seemed so much as to remark her distress; and I am ashamed to say that I ran among the rest. I was so weary that I had twice to make a halt and set down my bundles in the hundred yards or so between the pier and the railway station, so that I was quite wet by the time that I got under cover. There was no waiting-room, no refreshment-room; the cars were locked; and for at least another hour, or so it seemed, we had to camp upon the draughty, gas-lit platform."

The June day that my trio prepared to board the train for points west may not have been so wet and breezy, but the rush and confusion would be much the same.

Several days later, partway across country after an overnight stay at an emigrant hotel, Stevenson relates the experience of boarding the train, likely shared by my trio:

"I found myself in front of the Emigrant House, with more than a hundred others, to be sorted and boxed for the journey. A white-haired official, with a stick under one arm, and a list in the other hand, stood apart in front of us, and called name after name in the tone of a command. At

THE PRINCESS DOLL'S SCRAPBOOK

each name, you would see a family gather up its brats and bundles and run for the hindmost of the three cars that stood awaiting us, and I soon concluded that this was to be set apart for the women and children. The second or central car…was devoted to men travelling alone, and the third to the Chinese.

"I suppose the reader has some notion of an American railroad-car, that long, narrow wooden box, like a flat-roofed Noah's ark, with a stove and a convenience (toilet), one at either end, a passage down the middle, and transverse benches upon either hand.

"Those destined for emigrants on the Union Pacific are only remarkable for their extreme plainness, nothing but wood entering in any part into their constitution, and for the usual inefficacy of the lamps, which often went out and shed but a dying glimmer even while they burned.

"The benches are too short for anything but a young child. Where there is scarce elbowroom for two to sit, there will not be space enough for one to lie. Hence the company…conceived a plan for the better accommodation of travelers. They prevail on every two to chum together. To each of the chums they sell a board and three square cushions stuffed with straw, and covered with thin cotton.

The benches can be made to face each other in pairs, for the backs are reversible. On the approach of night the boards are laid from bench to bench, making a couch wide enough for two, and long enough for a man of the middle height; and the chums lie down side by side upon the cushions with the head to the conductor's van and the feet to the engine. When the train is full, of course this plan is impossible, for there must not be more than one to every bench; neither can it be carried out unless the chums agree."[47]

© CANSTOCK INC/HANKPIX. AS MARIA'S OCEAN TRIP BEGAN, MAY 10, 1869, NEW YORK HARBOUR WAS THE SCENE OF A CELEBRATION FOR THE COMPLETION OF THE TRANSCONTINENTAL RAILWAY.

The Transcontinental Railroad joined the east to the west coast and marked the end of the glory

47   *"Traveling on an Emigrant Train, 1879"* EyeWitness to History, www.eyewitnesstohistory.com (2006) used with permission

days of Mississippi steamboat travel and the mighty river's role as the dividing point of east and west. The railroad made the opening of homesteading land less dangerous and time consuming as compared to wagon train travel that averaged ten miles a day. Based on Stevenson's story our trio made it to their destination in under a week. Compare that with their earlier families' experiences on the canals and lakes.

Maria and her siblings travelled the Union Pacific line, but was it to Chicago, or a point in southeastern Iowa? I read again the Anchor line ad for the trip, shown in Chapter Eight; it was to Chicago. The last lap of their train journey was on the Chicago, Milwaukee, St Paul & Pacific line. This rail line had not reached their final destination, Decorah, until late 1869; it ended at Ossian, six miles southeast of there. Their brother, Hans, arriving three months later, listed Ossian, Iowa as his destination on *The Toten Emigrant* site. The last and shortest leg of their journey was by stagecoach, unless their family met them there.

Their destination reached, what a happy reunion it must have been! It had been eight years since they had said their farewells to Bertha. Their young brother, Laurits, was born seven months after that. Now, they met other new family members: their first brother-in-law, Ole Espe, and their nephews, Christian and Julius who were only three and four years younger than their *Oncle* Laurits, I imagined this was a cause for great fun and teasing. Maria, herself a twin, met her twin nieces, the toddlers, Jenny and Nelly, not yet two.

Glad reunions aside, challenges lay ahead: a new land, a new language to learn, countless adjustments. What opportunities awaited? Were they up for it?

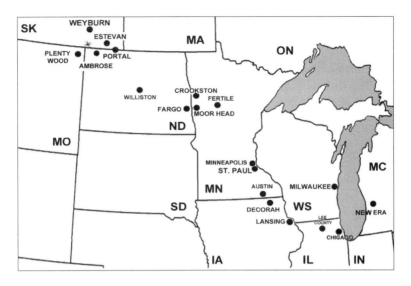

POINTS ALONG THE WAY[48]

48   This image is a portion of a North American map ©CanstockInc./ /JonnyCloud. Places marked on the map are approximate, photoshopped byMarlene Atkinsen. Homestead location marked with a star.

Part Four

THE IMMIGRANTS

Chapter Ten

PRINCESS STARTS
SOMETHING NEW

Though filled with typing errors, mistakes and corrections, it was so valuable. It was all I had—five typewritten pages telling my great-grandparents' Maria and Johan's story.

Thanks to Maria's oldest son, Jens, one line inspired this doll's story. I remembered Jens Gronvold (1880-1969) and his wife from annual fall visits in the early 1950s; Jens was a tall, soft-spoken, gangly man—with a squinty eye, just like his father had—and his wife, Mathilda, was plump, friendly, and engaging. Jens was my great-uncle, my grandmother's oldest brother. He had written this story of his mother, Maria, and father, Johan J. Gronvold, around 1965.

Several errors had sent me looking in the wrong places: *1866* should have been *1869*; the Espe family lived *east*, not *west* of Decorah; Winneshiek was the name of the county when the area referred to was Washington Prairie—also the name given to the church there. Additionally, my great-uncle did not have the contacts I had, thanks to the internet and the extensive research possibilities it offers.

Philip Ramstad, my fourth cousin, commented, "None of these are critical errors in such a narrative." Here, he was speaking of the nature of similar errors in his family's "House of Lovbraaten" story. "They are quite minor and serve to help us understand that the important thing in oral history is the feel of the past, not precision about dates and ages."

***

Jens wrote,

> "Karine, Laurits and mother (Maria) came to Decorah, Iowa in [1869]. Her sister, Bertha and husband Ole Espe were living in [Washington Prairie, east of] Decorah. Mother made her home with her sister when she was not working. Maria had employment in different households including Sanford and Anundsen. Sometimes in harvest time, she worked in the fields tying and shocking grain; they had no self-binders at that time. The wages were about \$2.00 and \$2.50 a day."

***

Decorah was a thriving town when Maria and her sister and brother arrived. The "1853 rush" described earlier told of large numbers of Norwegian people coming into the area. In the early 1860s, the establishment of the school, Luther College, followed close on the heels of the organization of congregations and churches (much like they did in Canada). Maria's uncle Hans was an early supporter, donating the sum of fifty dollars—a substantial amount for that time.

ELAINE MELBY AYRE

PERSPECTIVE MAP OF DECORAH, IOWA, NOT DRAWN TO SCALE.
"LOOKING NORTH WEST."
INCLUDES ILLUSTRATIONS AND INDEX TO POINTS OF INTEREST[49]

Maria's sister, Bertha, along with her husband and family, had not been there for very long when Maria arrived. First, I guessed their sudden move to Decorah, Iowa, from Lee County in north central Illinois happened in 1868 because the twins, Jenny and Nelly, were

---

49   Ruger, A. *Decorah, Winneshiek County, Iowa. 1870* Madison, Wis., Ruger &
      Stoner [1870] Col. Map 47 X 56 Cm, Library of Congress, *Geography and Map
      Division.* URL http://www.loc.gov/item/73693393 (accessed Oct 21, 2013)
      "Bird's eye" and perspective maps can be found of many towns and cities in the
      USA from this time period.

born in October 1867 in Illinois; I factored in the time for letters to be exchanged between Bertha, in Iowa, telling her family in Norway that they had moved, and Maria in Norway, letting Bertha know when they were coming. Finally, a spring 1868 baptismal record for the twins from Iowa confirmed Bertha and Ole had been there not much more than a year.

Following the Norwegian naming pattern, the girls were christened Gyda Katherine and Ragnhild Elizabeth. But on the 1870 census and for the rest of their lives, they were Jenny and Nelly.

***

A trip to the gold fields of California kick-started the Espe family's emigration/immigration story in America. A book written by Barbara Bulman related the family story of her father, John K. Hansen, founder of the Winnebago Company. Researching her family's background in Norway revealed Espe gold field finds were responsible for her ancestor's emigration to America. Therefore, a section about the Espes became part of her book. A photocopy of that chapter, shared with me, was my source of information about the Espe family.

> Peter and Elias Espe, older brothers of Bertha's husband, Ole, went to the Lee County area of Illinois in 1857. Times were tough financially. They barely earned enough to eat, working as farm laborers. Then Peter and Elias, along with other individuals from Bradford Township of Lee County, hearing about an 1859 Gold Strike in Colorado set out on foot with ox teams and covered wagons. That Pike's Peak gold strike turned out to be a bust! Their party broke up once they got as far as Nevada; some returned home, but four others, including Elias and Peter, continued on to California to try their luck in the gold fields there.

At one time, their food supply was very low. They only had some beans when they met someone who had salt; the two combined made a meal.

Coming across a wagon train massacre along the way, they buried the bodies before travelling on.

After six months travelling cross-country, they finally crossed over the Sierra Mountains into California. It was October, just before winter set in. They worked along the rivers in the mountains of Northern California for five years before returning home to Illinois. "Gold" financed the establishment of their farms and provided the means to bring their immediate and extended family over from their home on a steep hill, high above the famed Hardanger fjord, on Norway's southwestern coast.

Gary Krahenbuhl retraced that trip in 2009, on the 150th anniversary of the trip taken by his great-grandfather, Elias Espe. Then, he wrote and self-published *Travelling West in the Search for Gold in 1859: The Story of Peter L Govig, Peter O. Hill, Peter O. Espe and Elias O. Espe.* He recreated their trip west with photos and pictures, along with stories gathered from published sources telling of places visited by gold-seeking travellers into California so long ago. His recent research (since writing the booklet) revealed Elias and Peter returned to Illinois by a service provided by the Central America Transit Company. This involved taking the steamship, Moses Taylor, from San Francisco to Nicaragua. Originally it was thought they came across the isthmus at Panama, until actual ship's passenger records were found indicating that, after crossing Nicaragua, they sailed from San Juan del Norte (in Nicaragua) to NYC on the Golden Rule. After arriving in New York January 6, 1865, the trip back to Illinois was completed by train.

An interesting side note: the third member of this group, Peter O. Hill, married Peter and

Elias's only sister, Aasa Espe. Two brothers in this family were named Ole—"Big Ole" was the older; "Little Ole", the younger one, married my great-great aunt Bertha. Now, why would there be two sons with the same name? Likely because of Norwegian naming customs, and that *both* of their grandfathers were named Ole.

Knowing Bertha's Aunt Mari and family lived in Yorkville Prairie, south of Milwaukee, this would be the obvious place for Bertha to come. Since her ship landed at Quebec City, a good part of her trip inland would have been via the Great Lakes. No one seems to know how, when, or where Ole and Bertha's paths came to cross, though I eventually found that Ole had emigrated in 1857, the same year as his brothers.

* * *

Now, there was this odd occurrence regarding "little Ole", an example of immigrants dealing with ethnic rivalry. Ole bought a horse from an Irishman. When Ole discovered the animal suffered from moon blindness, he confronted the seller to state his objections. Later, the seller showed up with friends to back him up. A fight took place. Ole obviously held his ground against the gang, but so concerned about possible consequences, he packed his young family up and left that very night.

They journeyed over to Decorah, a distance of about 170 miles, where Bertha had relatives. Averaging ten to fifteen miles a day, such a trip took at least two weeks.

The 1870 census and Plat map showed Bertha and Ola Espe were living on an eighty acre farm, a couple miles southeast of Decorah. Their children—Christian, born in 1864, Julian, born in 1865, and the twins, Jenny and Nelly, born in 1867—had all been born in Lee County, in north central Illinois. Their seventeen-year-old Uncle Hans was living with them. Hans Kristiansen had left Norway in September 1869 the previous fall. He was their hired man (but I knew he was Bertha and Maria's brother). A few miles away was the farm of their aunt and uncle, Neils and Anne Mathea Voldeng and beyond that another couple miles east into the adjoining Allamakee County was uncle Hans and aunt Martha's farm and to the south her cousin, Kjersti and Johannes Husebye. Though I studied the Decorah census line by line, I never found Maria (or Karine) during the time she spent in this area, except to find that she and her brother, Hans, were sponsors at the baptism of her sister Bertha's third son, Olaf, born October 1870; the only documentation found to prove she was there, other than Jens's story. (Bertha's fourth son, Albert, was born two years later, also in October.)

***

A line in Jens's story inferred Maria had an offer of marriage from an employer whose wife had died in childbirth (for that was common, and that was how her sister, Karine, met her mate). Somehow Jens had the mistaken idea that it was the well-known Anundsen, editor of *Decorah Posten,* Maria could have married. It didn't take too much searching to learn that B. Anundsen's wife did not die until 1903 so Jens's presumption was incorrect. Undoubtedly, *Decorah Posten* was well read in the Gronvold household and perhaps it can be explained by the underlying human desire to find connections to those who are well known.

However, the phrase, Maria "...preferred Johan from the store," inspired my theory, years before I found the proof as to the doll's origins. Maria's brother, Hans, may also have worked in that store. I imagined the start of her relationship with Johan was a combination of her brother's encouragement, and checking out the doll. Sometime before she married Johan in May 1876, she bought that doll and gave it to Jenny and Nelly. My best guess- it was when the twins celebrated their eighth birthday in 1875.

Though the doll played a role in Maria and Johan's courtship, Princess remains silent on the details.

***

I gathered up my nerve and decided I could manage all that driving myself. With my Princess doll in tow, a family history journey became a reality in October 2009. I stayed at a bed and breakfast on the east end of Water Street (Main Street) in Decorah, and spent an evening poring over a history book celebrating 150 years of the Washington Prairie Lutheran Church.

I was particularly interested in the 1870 decade; there, I found lists of confirmation students—among them Maria's younger cousins from two families, as well as her nephew, Christian Espe, in the year 1878, when he was fifteen. His brother, Julius' name on a separate 1882 list made me wonder. Had he attended a class but moved before he was confirmed?

Travelling to Decorah, almost twenty-five hundred kilometers from my Alberta home, offered an opportunity to experience, for a brief moment, the place this family had lived. Where Ole and Bertha Espe had farmed for more than ten years was now the local airport. I came past the hanger and stood at the edge of the airstrip.

Here was where Bertha, Maria, Karine, Laurits, Anton and Hans reconnected after leaving Norway.

And Jenny and Nelly spent pleasant childhood days here playing with their Princess doll. Experiencing those few minutes there meant a lot to me, for this location represented the treasured beginnings of Princess's story.

**

The property at the height of land had a view of the countryside spreading out toward the south. If the homestead buildings had stood there, I realized they could look out the window and see the spire of the Washington Prairie Lutheran Church less than two miles away. The church stood out as a symbol of hope and encouragement—a testimony to the importance their Christian faith played in those Norwegian immigrants' lives.

Washington Prairie Lutheran Church

This was the first Lutheran church established west of the Mississippi River in 1853 by the Reverend U. V. Koren. He came from Norway as a recent Seminary graduate with his new wife, Elisabeth. Development of the area was just beginning. Elisabeth Koren, from an upper-class Norwegian family, was very different from the poorer lower-class immigrants scrambling to make a go of their homesteads. She wrote of her experiences over the first couple of years in a book titled *The Diary of Elisabeth Koren*. The tireless Koren travelled over a wide area of northeast Iowa and south central Minnesota, preaching and establishing new Lutheran congregations.

The Korens were a talented couple, and widely respected. I discovered a hymn I liked was written by U. Koren, as well as many poems included in the Washington Prairie Church History book.

***

In addition, this was where Bertha and her children experienced their greatest loss: in July 1879, Ole, the head of the family, died after a short-term illness. Brain fever, the disease's name in those days, was a death sentence. Even today, this viral disease, called spinal meningitis, is a challenge for medical treatment.

They now faced life without their husband, father, and breadwinner. Fortunately the two oldest boys were essentially adults. Christian, born in 1864, and Julian, born in 1865, led their family on an ox-cart journey from Decorah to a place in Norman County in 1881, southwest of Polk County where Maria, Karine, and their families had moved the year before. With Ole gone and none of his family close by, I felt sure the move was made so Bertha could be closer to her own immediate family—three brothers, Hans, Anton and Laurits, and her sisters, Maria and Karine, who all lived in west central Minnesota. This new area afforded more opportunities for her four sons.

In 1885, Jenny turned eighteen and married Knut Bragestad who also moved up from Decorah, Jenny and her family likely knew him before.

Her twin sister, Nelly died as a young woman within the next ten years. [Maybe that explains why my Mother's pony was Nelly.]

***

And the jostling about on the ox-cart journey might explain how the Princess doll was crushed, breaking off her back shoulder. A length of haywire served the purpose of keeping the doll's head on the body. By now, the twins—just into their early teens—had a four-year-old cousin, Maria's daughter, Ragna, to whom they intend to give their doll.

Chapter Eleven

HOMESTEADING TALES

Now that Maria had Johan in her life we learn about his background:[50]

> "Johan was born in January 1849 to Jens Larsen, the hired man (or *husman*), who was permanently employed; he furnished a house and raised a family there. He did not own a farm. The farm, called Thorpestuen, was located in Hedmark, Norway, the region between Oppland and the Swedish border. [His name should have been Johan Jensen Thorpe—we have no idea how he picked the name Gronvold.] He had two brothers and two sisters.
>
> He came to the United States in 1870 and worked in New York as a longshoreman, to earn enough for the balance of his journey and left for Decorah, Iowa the same year. There is where he was acquainted with Maria. He worked at a variety of jobs: a carpenter building barns, a mail carrier, a store clerk and tying and shocking grain in the harvest fields."

In May of the American Centennial year, 1876, Maria and Johan were married. They bought an eighty-acre farm across the Minnesota border in Mower County, about twenty miles from Austin. Two or three crop failures later, they gave up the farm. Why they were at a farm in

---

50   Jens's Story

Bennington Township at the eastern edge of Mower County was a puzzle to me. One answer revealed after several hours at the Genealogical Library for Mower County in Austin, Minnesota- Pastor U.V. Koren had organized Bloomfield Lutheran Church just inside the border of adjoining Fillmore County. It was close enough, I speculated, that it could have been where they went to church. Much later in my research, I learned three of Maria's oldest cousins from her Aunt Mari's family (Juel, Paul and Evan Hansen Skari—and two of their married sisters) were early settlers on the western edge of Fillmore County. I thought that was the family connection until I found an even closer connection.

There was the matter of Maria and Johan's close-by neighbor—Ole and Carrie Rud, with seven children, recorded just above Maria and Johan on the 1880 census. I dismissed the possibility Carrie was Maria's sister, Karine when I saw the oldest child had been born before Karine arrived. Finally, a census from 1885, I had missed finding before, showed it was indeed Maria's sister, Karine.

Since all the Rud children were born in Minnesota, Ole Rud had lived in this area before. I checked with Sue at the Mower County Historical Society at Austin MN, Ole's name was not attached to any land. His first wife had died, and Karine became his second wife; maybe that was why Johan and Maria settled there to begin with. The 1900 census stated, Karine had been married twenty-five years, so that put her there in 1875, the year before Johan and Maria married. Somehow, I wondered if there had been an earlier connection between Johan and Ole.

***

What plague sent them on their way? Having knowledge of some of them via Laura Ingalls Wilder's books relating this same period, I knew how devastating they were for homesteaders of that era, and later. Was it a hailstorm wiping out a bumper wheat crop, or an outbreak of grasshoppers? A newspaper item in the Bloomfield church history, referred to earlier, revealed something I had never heard of.

ELAINE MELBY AYRE

And the Washington Prairie Church History retold, "In the latter part of the 1870s, the region was plagued by 'chinch bugs' and the wheat crop failed year after year."[51]

His name, J.J. Gronvold, set in bold type, on the list of unpaid taxes in a column of a local Mower County newspaper for both 1881 and 1882 spoke volumes. He had vacated his property. [This reminded me of a story told of my Grandpa Melby's Dirty Thirties experience fifty years later. In his total frustration, he dropped off the deed to his land at the Land titles office as he was on his way north, saying, "You can have it."]

This was only a continuation of Johan's bad luck, for before they settled in eastern Mower County, Jens related:

> "Father had loaned $800.00 to a farmer and when he could not pay him he gave father a deed to a farm in South Dakota. When he went to look up the place, someone that had acquired the farm on a tax deed lived there. Father had sent the money for the taxes on the place to a lawyer and he skipped with the money."

This is an example of how crooked officials sometimes took advantage of immigrants. It sounded to me like more gloom heaped upon increasing misery.

***

The spot where they had lived was simple to locate on the grid roads, laid out on mostly flat land, with mile after mile of cornfields. A short distance to the west was a line of innumerable wind generators (that extend across the states, south all the way to Texas). Johan had the forty acres on both the northeast and northwest side of the 170 Ave and 150 Street crossroad where I stopped. On the southeast corner, a clump of trees marked the location of Norby School, where at least three or four of the Rud children went to school.

***

---

51   Myhre, Elaine A. *The Story of Washington Prairie and the Land Beyond 1800-2002* Anundsen Publishing Co Decorah, IA. p.148

The Pioneers

Standing beside their oxen
They came a valiant band
Traveling by covered wagon
Bound for the Promised Land

The wagons bore a heavy load
All space could well allow
Hung at the rear the water kegs,
At the side the breaking plow.

Behind the wagons, the children walked,
The sheep, the pigs and kine,
The faithful dogs brought up the rear
To keep the stock in line.

Their goal was in Polk County
Their path the ox-cart trail,
Free land, free for the choosing,
To be bought by a life of toil.

When the wagons rolled by Frenchman's Bluff
The tired travelers reckoned
Beyond the prairies to the North,
The Sand Hill Valley beckoned.

The vanguard came in '79
In '80 came a host
In '81 the balance came
And so the deal was closed.

Many came up from Iowa
In Polk their fates to share
The chinch bug and the hoppers,
Had wiped them out down there.

The Irish and the Yankees
Were fated not to stay,
Their choice of land was very poor,
The topsoil blew away.

From Norway and from Sweden
They came across the sea,
Their friends had first informed them,
This was the place to be.

From southern Minnesota
A goodly number came
To the Sand Hill River Valley
The virgin land to tame.

The toil was hard, the years slipped by,
The goal at last seemed near
But Father Time is pitiless
For some the cost was dear.

The fruit of all their work is here
For everyone to see
So hail the sturdy Pioneers
Who caused it all to be.

The pioneers have slumbered long,
Their work is done and well
Our task remain, in some small way,
Their story now to tell.

By Edward Torpet[52]

---

52   From- Bolstad K., Dale H., Torpet E. Editors *Garfield-The first 100 years 1880-1980* Used by permission of Torpet family.

Red River Carts loaded with furs trapped throughout the central Canadian plains made their way to market via the Mississippi River starting at St Paul, Minnesota and brought needed supplies back to the settlements around Winnipeg from the early 1800s. Those ox-cart trains with as many as one hundred noisy, squeaky carts definitely left a trail. But by 1880 railroads took over from ox-carts; the trails became a route for the homesteaders coming to central Minnesota.

Thinking of the ox-cart trail as being the route my family travelled intrigued me. As I began my initial research, I learned of Orlin Ostby who followed the Pembina trail with his teenage son and daughter, his ox, Pum pulling the authentic ox-cart he constructed. Their trip took them from northwest Minnesota down to the State Fair to commemorate the 150th anniversary of the state of Minnesota in 2008.

Meeting some of Ostby's friends and family was another bonus of my family history trip.

***

Great-grandmother Maria's cousin, Kjersti was closest in age to her but before Maria was married and getting established in Mower County, Kjersti and Johannes Husebye had six children. According to a 1949 letter from Phillip Ramstad's great-uncle, Henry was one of those six, remembering back 70 years to those homesteading days. His father, Johanes thought their little farm, south of Decorah, was too small to keep them all, so he decided to go and "see the great west and broad Red River Valley, where ... some cousins ... had moved 1871, and reported how it looked and thought it would become all right when it would get a railroad and more people, as there [was] lots of good flat land for homesteading at low prices."

"So in the spring of 1878...he bought some good land, bargained for some more, and in the spring of 1879 he rented out the farm in Iowa. Then father started for Fargo with a carload of eight horses and farm machinery, including a new McCormick five foot wire binder still in the crate.

A boy about 16, named Laurits Christianson Blaavarp, who was mother's cousin, came with father to work for him that summer, but had gone to his brother Hans at Lake Park, Minnesota, for the winter by the time we arrived in Fargo about the middle of November." (Hans and Laurits were two of Maria's younger brothers; Laurits was the youngest brother who had come to America with her. The first time I found Laurits, listed as Lewis, with Hans and Martha's family in the 1870 census, so this was where he lived as his sisters were out working.)

Henry describes the family's first trip to the homestead "over the unbroken prairie from lower Front Street almost a straight line southwest to Norman, and we only passed one farm house some miles out of Fargo, a French family living in two rooms, [a] sod house [with] one room for the people and one for the livestock. We met a few farmers heading for Fargo, all driving with oxen. We were driving with horses. [There wasn't] room in the wagon, so some had to walk. Starting from Moorhead about 10:00

a.m., we arrived at Jacob Shelver's at Norman about 4:00 p.m., where we stayed overnight and were very well taken care of, though they were a family of about the same size as ours. Their house was a two room log house with a low attic with bark and sod roof, but it accommodated about 16 - the two families.

Next day we drove another three miles northwest to the southeast corner of school section one half mile north of the house that became our home, but there was an old log house on the school section where we had to make a temporary home for about a week till ours could be somewhat fitted up so we could move in, [though it] was not hardly fit to live in for [that]... cold and stormy winter....

Father, of course, had had too much work to do that summer and fall to get everything in tip top shape for us, but had done very well as it was, but he had the crop threshed, plowing done, lumber hauled all the way from Fargo about 25 miles to build the house 16 x 24 x 12 high. The plate and lumber for a well and small granary, but had had no time to put up anything for the eight horses, so had to do it after we arrived, and go to the river to get fire wood for the winter. He had a man help him haul wood and build a straw stable, had to make some more trips to Fargo for more supplies, but at that, we did not get storm sashes or doors nor hardly any banking around the walls, so the potatoes froze. He had a man dig a well fourteen feet and got four feet of water, so face a Dakota winter with what we had to eat and live on that winter. We would never try again. No cows, pigs or chickens, no fresh meat, milk, eggs, or vegetables, just white flour bread, some frozen potatoes, some salt side pork and some butter and only 25 miles of blockaded roads to town with food stores and no canned food even there. But I remember Father did shoot two jackrabbits and made me a trap with which I caught a few birds, so we did get a taste of fresh meat.

The weather was not so bad till after Christmas, but from then till about April it was bad with lots of snow, so much that when it melted, the Cheyenne, Wild Rice and Red Rivers flooded over all low lands and that happened for the three years 1880-81-82. Father's land was high and dry and crops were good, but low land was no good. However, we were happy when the snow commenced to melt and the wild geese and ducks commenced to fly north, though we got only the honk.

Also Laurits Christianson also came back from Lake Park to work for us, and Father got a chance to buy an old cow... that gave a small amount of milk and we thought we never had tasted anything as good as milk and bread. Soon he got a chance at another cow or two and some pigs and chickens and Mother... planted some garden vegetables and ... we started to live.

The wheat and oats and a few potatoes were about the only crops that were... put in and a fence was put up around about 50 acres for pasturing horses and cows and about 60 or 70 acres more broke up out of the three quarters that Father had bought in that section, and the rest was used for hay meadow, and that year the crops turned out good, 25 to 30 bushels per acre, and during that summer of 1880 the... railroad line was graded, track built.. the railroad bridge was built late in the fall, so the track and first train reached Kindred at Christmas."

***

Meanwhile, following a trend, Ole Rud and Johan Gronvold left Bennington Township of Mower County for Polk County, Minnesota. Jens thought Johan may have come up on a scouting trip in late '79 driving with horses. Johan's name was on that June 2, 1880 census of Mower County, though he likely was away getting his homestead in Polk County prepared. Maria came up in August 1880 by train to Ada about forty miles from the homestead, along with Johnnie, Ragna and her sister, Mrs. Ole Rude, and Ole's sister, Helene. Jens made no mention of Ole and Karine's family of seven.

Reading this, I presumed Johnnie was Karine, Mrs. Ole Rude's child—but after rechecking the 1880 census, listed below three-year-old Ragna, the last entry on the page, is a John C. with a line crossed through it. The Johnnie in this document could be the child missing in the 1900 census where it states Maria had seven children—but only the five born in Polk County survived. Johnnie likely died as an infant soon after the move to Polk County.

> "Johan and Ole drove to [Ada to the train to] meet them, they drove with oxen, a very fast [mode of] transportation. [Jens's humor!] [Maria was pregnant and] it was still a two-day trip back to the homestead near Fertile. The homestead was about twenty-five miles south of Crookston, a wild and wooly city in the Red River Valley. Johan had filed squatter's right to 160 acres, but the land office let Kari Bromberg take one forty. Johan did not go to court about it; no doubt, he

did not have the money. This was in the summer when he was working on the Martin Johnson Farm."

©CanStockPhotoInc/AlexanderZam

Their homestead was a dugout with two rooms built into the east facing side of a hill above a small slough maybe something like the image on this stamp. The back room served as a root cellar and storage; the front room served as living room, kitchen, and bedroom. The walls were round logs, and the roof was birch bark and dirt. The far end of the roof was even with the ground. It had only one window and one door. Three sons were born here: Jens in 1880 (in late November after the big move), Henry in 1883, and Adolph in 1885.

After living in this dugout for five years, Maria and Johan's family numbered six. They moved into a new two-story house on the hill, where my grandmother, Dina Amelia, was born October 2, 1887, in Garfield Township, Polk County; she was the sixth of seven children born to Maria and Johan Gronvold. Several years after Dina, her youngest brother, Olaf, was born in 1890.

"The new house had one room downstairs, one room upstairs, and a root cellar. The walls were hewn logs with mortised or dovetailed corners, a very good construction. After a year or so, a kitchen was built and both had shingle roofs."[53]

In 1988, Mel Roragen, an old-timer from Fertile took my mother and I to see where this original Gronvold homestead had been a couple miles southeast of the town of Fertile, MN. As we stood there, my mother remembered Grandma's comment on seeing this place as an adult. As a child, Grandma thought the slough at the bottom of the hill was a lake!

***

It was helpful to discover a copy of *Garfield-The First 100 Years-1880-1980* among my mother's papers, for that township had been Gronvold's location for twenty-five years. On Sept 13, 1880, about forty settlers in the community held a township organizational meeting and chose to name their township after the current Republican candidate for the presidency. (President Garfield held four months in office when he was injured in an assassination attempt. He was unable to govern, though he lived another eighty days).

It is interesting to see how they managed to build roads. With money in short supply, each male inhabitant was assessed two days highway labour. There were nine road overseers for the township, charged with the responsibility of getting each man to work off his two days. Both Johan Gronvold and his brother-in-law, Ole Rud, took turns as overseers during this time.[54]

***

An organizational meeting was held on July 6, 1880 for the congregation, Little Norway Church. Johan was busy working, getting his homestead prepared for Maria's arrival, so his name is not among the charter

---

53   From Jens's Story about Maria and Johan

54   Bolstad K., Dale H., Torpet E. Editors *Garfield-The first 100 years 1880-1980* Publisher not mentioned, 48 pages , p. 11-12

members. The Little Norway Congregation 75th anniversary souvenir booklet states that when the first church was built in 1882, it was on the southeast corner of section 15, Anders Morvig's farm, kitty corner from Gronvold's property (section 23). (Jens became Anders Morvig's son-in-law when he married his daughter, Mathilda, in 1908.)

Johan is listed as one of the two who built that 24x36 log church building. This structure was only half-finished in 1883 when another piece of land was given to the congregation, this time on the northeast corner of section 15 (which was divided by the winding Sand Hill River much like it divided the township). So the log church was dismantled and reassembled on the site of the present church with the addition of a 12x12 sacristy. Within ten years, an entirely new church was built.[55]

* * *

A temporary Ladies Aid was organized in 1882 and its organizers were Mrs. Ole Christiansen and Mrs. Johan Gronvold.[56] Their project was the making of an altar covering for the church.

I wondered, "Was this a memorial project for Maria's son, Johnnie?"

But I do know for sure, that sometime the year they moved, Maria got the news of her mother, Ragnhild's death, back in Norway.

Our forebears were determined to provide their children with the basic principles of Christian Education. Starting in 1882, Parochial School was held for two months in the summer.

The Old Norwegian custom of men sitting on the right side of the aisle and the women and children on the left side was abolished in 1899. Families were permitted to sit together, but it took a generation before the custom completely discontinued.

---

55 *75th Anniversary Diamond Jubilee Edition July 9-10, 1955*, Little Norway Congregation, Garfield Township, Polk County, Minnesota. 47 pages, p7

56 *75th Anniversary Diamond Jubilee Edition July 9-10, 1955*, Little Norway Congregation, Garfield Township, Polk County, Minnesota. 47 pages, p11

Little Norway Church
Fertile, Minnesota
75th Anniversary - 1955

Little Norway Lutheran Church
Fertile, Minnesota
1880 - 100th Anniversary - 1980

57

---

57   Log church from 75th Anniversary Booklet mentioned in previous footnote
      combined in a collage by Marlene Atkinsen with my photos of the plates that

ELAINE MELBY AYRE

Ragna was ten years old and happy to welcome a sister when Dina Amelia was born in 1887. A baby sister was even better than her precious Princess doll.

Then, Ragna became another victim of the dreaded brain fever. Dina would hardly have been able to remember, for she was only a few months over a year old when her big sister died in January of 1889. A lovely tombstone commemorates Ragna Oline, 1877-1889, at the Little Norway Lutheran Church cemetery.

"It must have been hard for mother to lose her girl at that age," Dina comments in a two-page handwritten "Story of My [Early] Life."

Because her family was so hard up, they did not have as nice things (clothes and shoes) as others. Consequently, they lived simply and did not go out much, the main reason I believed Grandma's doll was a hand-me-down. That did not make the doll any less special to her. Even though she had not been able to tell me any of the details I longed to know, I recognized the doll was a precious and real connection to her sister, Ragna Oline.

* * *

An older brother of her father—her uncle Lars—his wife, Anna Spangen, and son, Mathias, had immigrated in 1881. This cousin of Dina's married the sister of the first minister to serve Little Norway Church after its organization, before Dina was around.

Dina remembered, "We sure were happy when *Oncle* Lars rewarded us with a sugar lump when we brought them their mail."

Dina said that her mother was happiest when her oldest brother Jens read from the Bible. In those years, that Bible likely was the only book in the household. This Bible inscribed *Johan Jensen Gronvold 1876* on the inside front cover made me wonder, "Had it been a wedding present?

once hung in Grandma's living room

In old style Gothic script, its pages yellowed and falling apart, it was worse for wear after it was knocked off our mantel (when the mirror above our fireplace crashed to the floor several years ago).

Looking at Ole and Karine Rud family's birth and death dates tells a story. The 1900 census states Karine had been married 25 years, she was the mother of the children born after 1875.

-Ole Rud 1847-1901 and Karine 1848-1927
-Petra 1869-1893 (24)
-John Adolf 1870-1947
-Lena 1871-1960
-Anna 1874-1895 (21)
-Oscar O. 1876-1898 (22)
-Mary 1877 -1884? (6 or 7)
-Claus 1879-1881 (2)
-Clause 1881-1885 (4)
-Maria Louise 1884-after 1910 (25+)
-Claus Olaf 1885-?
-Clara Henrietta 1887-1907 (20)
-Nora Ovidia 1890-1973 -Albert 1892-1960

Note how many died young. A final blow for Dina was to hear that her special cousin, Clara had died Nov 7, 1907. She stayed with Clara, where she worked at a Crookston Hotel before the Gronvolds left Fertile in 1906. The hand-written death card for Clara sadly explains- "Pulmonary Tuberculosis-a Family Weakness"

[58]

Dina considered her cousins (Karine's daughters) to be her best friends, especially Clara, only two months younger than she was. Maria, or Malla, was an older by a couple of years, and Nora, who Grandma

---

58   Minnesota Historical Society death card #1907-54-1934, from research done by Barb Raaen

kept in contact all through the years, was younger. Since they did not get out much, times of getting together with her cousins were special.

In spite of only three years of schooling, Dina could read and spell quite well. Some of her schooling was attending bible school for a month in the summer and "reading for the minister," the study of Luther's Catechism leading to Confirmation. In those times, in the eyes of congregation, confirmation gave the young person adult status.

Through all the families in those homesteading years:

> "When it became necessary for children ...to "go to the minister" to acquire their religious instruction, prepa-ratory to their confirmation at the age of fourteen or fifteen, they usually walked afoot [barefoot] across the rugged hills from their homes to the church.

> "In a little oilcloth bag, they carried their much-revered books of religious training, viz: catechism, *Forklaring* (book of explanation) and Bible History. These books were sacred and must be protected from the weather, as well as preserved for the use of other younger confir-mands to come."[59]

***

> "In 1900 we traded the farm for the old Valley post office and store (located at farthest southeast point of Garfield) where we built a feed mill with a four roller mill and a twelve horsepower gasoline engine. Father ran the feed mill. I managed the store, Henry was the farmer and Adolph was the helper. The store, building and farm belonged to Brown Duckstad, the hardware man in Fertile. We paid the stupendous sum of $7.00 a year rent for the building and we rented the farm for half. New shingles were put on and new sills were

---

59   Clarence Petersen *The House of Lovbraaten Decorah Public Opinion*, January 28, 1942 Used with permission. A description of the confirmation of Maria's Decorah cousin in 1867

put in. Not much profit for the landlord, was it?" Jens wrote.

Their financial situation seems to have improved.

GRONVOLD FAMILY PORTRAIT CA 1900. SEATED LEFT TO RIGHT OLAF, JOHAN, MARIA, DINA. STANDING ADOLPH, JENS, HENRY

ELAINE MELBY AYRE

Despite the fact that her mother, Maria, did not know how to sew, Dina taught herself. She made enough money to buy cloth by selling items she made with her knitting machine. That she made herself a special white dress for a Fourth of July celebration intrigued me. Her cousins from Gary were at the celebration in Fertile, and they had a good time she told in her "Life Story". Was this the dress she wore in her early portrait?

***

An advertisement[60] from that time presented this appealing information:

OPPORTUNITY!

THE GOLDEN CHANCE FOR YOUNG
BUSINESS MEN

IN NORTHERN WILLIAMS COUNTY —
THE GARDEN SPOT OF NORTH DAKOTA

A NEW TOWNSITE – ON THE
SOO LINE-NOW BUILDING

WE HAVE THE CLIMATE   AN ABUNDANCE OF COAL
WE HAVE THE FARMERS   GOOD HAY, GOOD WATER
WE HAVE THE BEST SOIL   GOOD CROPS & ROADS

CAST YOUR LINE IN A PLEASANT PLACE

LAWYERS   LANDMEN   DRUGGIST
BLACKSMITH   BARBER   SADDLER
CONFECTIONER   NURSERYMAN   COBBLER
PHOTOGRAPHER   WELL DIGGER   PAINTER
ANY OTHER LEGITIMATE BUSINESS

---

60   http://www.ambrosend.com/47-businesses.html *The Weekly Newsman*, Ambrose, N. D Friday, July 6, 1906 *From the Stories and Histories of Divide County* 1964. Note Williams County became Divide County

Six years after their move to Valley, with Dina's brothers interested in getting established on their own the family made another move. Was it based on this advertisement? Her folks set up a store in a new and developing area, along the northwestern border of the state of North Dakota at Ambrose; the boys went further west into the north eastern corner of Montana. But meanwhile the man who would be my grandfather was already on the move and writing about his emigration and immigration experiences in a diary.[61]

---

61   JOHN (JORDBRAEK) HANSEN'S DIARY: thin pocket diary with a small indelible pencil hidden in the binding was kept by my grandfather, John B. Hansen's during his 1903 emigration from Norway and his first 18 months in America. It was rediscovered when I stayed at my grandmother's place 1966-1968. Translated by my aunt, Myrtle Hansen in 2003, assisted by second cousins, Hermod and Bjorg Monsen of Skien, Norway, typed by cousin Wayne and Dolores Hagen and distributed to Hansen family members. Adapted version.

Chapter Twelve

JOHN'S EMIGRATION/ IMMIGRATION STORY

Forty years plus a day before I was born, my grandfather, John was up early to begin his emigrant journey from his home at Jordbraek, Skoger, Buskerud in Norway. He caught the 8 o'clock train from Drammen, arrived in Oslo at 11, paid for the ticket on his passage on the steam-ship <u>Hekla</u>, saw a doctor at 12 ("who only looked a bit in my mouth"), and reported at 5 to the Police Station, the usual procedure emigrants underwent before leaving the country.

He spent the afternoon with his cousin on his mother's side, Emilie and her husband Herman and had dinner at his Aunt Helle's place. A group of relatives saw him off before he boarded at 10:30. He went to bed but in his excitement, couldn't sleep.

> *"The boat left 22 May, 1903 at 10:15 a.m. in nice sunshine with music and dance from Xana. [Up till 1925, Oslo was called Kristiania.] Arrived here in Kristiansand at 3 o'clock so had plenty of time to look around where I have never been before and got to talk to my "nice" cousin, Andreas.*

> *The boat left again at 10:30 but by midnight the boat rocked and many were sick. 6 o'clock I had to vomit.*

> *24.5 [John wrote dates, Norwegian style- day, then month.] Today is nice but I am sick after the motion last night so I have been in my bed all day and have eaten nothing.*

25.5 The food is quite good but a person must be quick and grab for it or one will get nothing. Today I do not have much of an appetite and I regret that I didn't bring along with me some sour juice and salted meat. There must be many who are sick today because there are so few on the deck. [Nevertheless, conditions on 1900 Emigrant ships had improved even over when Maria travelled.]

26.5 People don't look very well. There is much fog this afternoon so the foghorn is heard quite often.

27.5 Nice weather. Don't feel well. Have eaten too little. Ate rather well for dinner, after having had some vegetables (???) That is something that everyone going to America should bring along to revive you. Today have only lukewarm water to drink. Saw the sunset.

28.5 Got some good Norwegian coffee from Stubson today and I feel better. Had melons with my meal at noon, which are good to avoid seasickness.

29.5 Have felt good today and have eaten well. One should bring along a little coffee pot, some coffee and sugar and some cream.

30.5 There has been a bit of fog in the night. I am well but it goes very slow. Will probably not arrive in New York until Thursday or Friday.

31.5 Pentecost. In the middle of the Atlantic. Nice weather, the sea is perfectly still.

1.6 Pentecost. It has rained a little today, but this evening it is especially nice. I am well, but it is a special Pentecost.

2.6 Not feeling too well. Feel better this afternoon maybe because of the nice weather and the moonshine.

ELAINE MELBY AYRE

3.6 Nice sunshine, weather warmer and warmer each day. Have today seen a two-masted steamer far to the right; also seen the sun which was completely red at sunset.

4.6 Has blown so much today so that the boat rocked quite a bit. I got sick this morning. Afternoon well again.

5.6 Especially nice weather. We surely will come to our destination early to-morrow.

6.6 Today I was up very, very early in order to be ready for landing which was not at all necessary as we would not arrive in New York till 4 pm (Norwegian time) The time change is 5:40 from Norway to New York and so we were 15 ¼ days on the sea. The first things I bought were apples, a large thick biscuit and juice. I ate these while the customs officials looked through all our clothes, which went quickly. After the custom clearance [at Ellis Island], we were put on a small boat and went across to Castle Garden where the doctor made a brief check again and we were asked various questions. We were divided into groups according to where we were going and we left in two separate boats. The boat I was on stopped near a place filled with packing boxes. There we were locked up in a room and the heat nearly killed us. We were here for 3 hours and we did not get on the train and leave from New York before 9 pm American time.

7.6 Came to Buffalo 9:00 am. We're driven by taxi a little way and I lost Gateren, my last Norwegian companion, who went in another taxi. I came to a train station and had to wait till 3:30 pm to leave and arrived in Detroit at 12 midnight.[62]

---

62   Twisted Twigs on Gnarled Branches Genealogy Facebook page explained it for me this way~ *theBuffaloTimes*,February1,1903 http://www.buffalohisto-ryworks.com/.../union-station.html "Buffalo has four railroad stations, the Central ... the Erie on the same thoroughfare, the LehighValley...,and the Lackawanna...."

8.6 Here I laid down in the train station and slept well. However, my voice got rather hoarse as I was laying on a cast iron plate under which there was some sort of steam heating, and above me was the cold air. Left from here at 8:20 am and arrived at Grand Rapids (Michigan) at 1:30pm. Left Grand Rapids at 5:30 pm. Arrived in New Era (Michigan) at 8:30 pm. I got a bed at the hotel and I slept remarkably well and I missed the meals.

9.6 Got up in great form and took my time looking around places in New Era. I finally [spoke] to Nordberg, an old Swedish man, who helped me out and accompanied me until I found my 2 young cousins, Ernest and Edgar Johnsen, who were bringing milk to the creamery and I got a lift with them to my uncle's place. It was with strange feelings that I went to this place. 12 o'clock noon I was given a good welcome by my uncle and aunt. I stayed with them the rest of the month. [John's aunt Jacobine, married to his mother's brother, Hartvig Johnsen, suggested he change his name from Jordbraek to Hansen. John's father's name was Bernhard Hansen Jordbraek, so that was how John picked the name, Hansen.]

One of the first days in July, I started working for Viktor Munson [at New Era, cultivating with a big red horse without lines in the tall corn.[63]] Got a dollar a day and I enjoyed myself. Worked like that for 14 days until arrangements were made with him to get $20 for 4 weeks. When this time was up, he had no more work for me to do and on the 25th of August, I went to Slocum, Michigan to get work [carrying lumber and later loading a trolley with newly sawed lumber.]

I worked for $1.30 a day until November 26 when I was unlucky, fell and broke one of my thumbs.

---

63   Some of this additional information was found in John's later handwritten memoir.

ELAINE MELBY AYRE

Was at the doctor on Nov. 26 and got it bandaged and again Nov. 28th in the morning, on my way back here. Was at Dr. Wilson on the 30th. He took off the bandages and made a new one and sent some with me so that I could change them every 3rd or 4th day. Today, the 7th Dec. it feels good. As soon as it is good again I'll go back to Slocum and stay there until spring at least.

9.12 Went to see the doctor today. We have a lot of snow. And he said all was well and that it was straight

12.12 However it looks as if it will be bent.

16.12 Today, it is quite straight

17.12 Everything ok, the weather is better.

19.12 Rain today. The snow might disappear.

Jenny Elida was born. (She was John's oldest brother, Hans's daughter)

20.12 Good weather. All is well.

22.12 Was in Shelby – bought things for Christmas, spent almost $15.00

24.12 Was to see the Christmas tree in the church tonight –it was nicely decorated.

25.12 Christmas Day. It has been quiet at home, no service today.

26.12 Second day of Christmas. Went to work at 2:00 p.m. The weather was awful so there were only a few people there. Tonight the weather is terrible.

27.12 Weather is nicer today but there is lots of snow. English affairs this morning. My finger now feels good.

28.12 Nice weather

29.12 Looks like worse weather – much to do today.

30.12 Andrine Johnson, my cousin, was married to Arthur Long this evening at 7:30. He is ill after having driven from Shelby in the terrible weather which we have had to-day and this afternoon in particular. It seemed almost impossible for guests to come but the house was full and everything went well. People left at 1 in the night.

[Andrine, aka Anne Marie, was Hartvig and Jacobine Johnsen's oldest daughter.]

31.12 Today it is nice weather again and there is much to do to return things that were borrowed.

[New Year's Day, 1904] Today nice weather. I have been to the church where I gave an offering and tonight to Karstad in the Womens' Club where they were dancing, ate well and everything was fine.

3.1 Sunday. Was at church for Sunday school and later at G. Thorsen's – also at young people's gathering in the evening.

4.1 Today I went to Slocum.

5.1 Didn't get my former job [at the sawmill?] back as had been promised but I think I will have to stay at the unpleasant handling factory where I started.

9.1 Today Sunday – nice weather. This week I worked 5 ¾ day from Tues. morning – I worked ¾ day during night

11.1 Have moved to Char's after having paid Krist Vaker $3.40 for well over a week's stay.

12.1 Began to eat here this morning and I feel well here. Last night, I bought a clock from Martin for $19.00

16.1 This week I have worked every day.

17.1 Today, I feel sick all over. Had too much alcohol before I went to bed and I had a lot of stomach pain all night.

18.1 Today I am a little better but feel as if I've been beaten and driven over.

19.1 Today sicker (vomited) therefore I've been staying away from work and stayed at home.

20.1 Am now better and working again. Yesterday I received a letter from D. Halvorsen and today I have sent a letter to C. Bentsen, in Chicago.

23.1 Today – snowy weather. Henrik is sick – hasn't eaten anything today. Letter from Bentsen. [Much better mail service than today?]

24.-31.1 Nothing of interest. Henrik well again.

1.2 Got my former job again loading lumber.

2–12.2 Have been quite well and perky. On the 9th a man got driven over by the train here in the yard and he died after half an hour. Yes, this should be an example for us to be more careful.

13.2 Worked today and am also going to work all night. It will be hard but I will earn 12-13 kroners in 24 hours.

14.2 In the night I got a severe stomach ache and it has continued today – likely got it from the hard candy I ate.

18.2 Four days it has been very cold, and our faces were nearly frozen stiff.

21.2 Better weather the last 2 days and all is well except that I have gotten a little pain in the tendon behind the left heel. Yesterday I loaded indoors in the mill.

28.2 Have loaded 4 days this week. Am a little stiff in the right middle finger in the morning, but feel a bit better now. The heel continues to hurt a little. Got 4 letters one day this week. Worked the night.

6.3 This week we've had every kind of weather with rain, snow, fog and also nice weather. Yes, at 3 pm it was raining, we had a thunderstorm with lightning so it was just terrible. A lot of the snow has disappeared. Have this week been quite well even if I have had a cold and people tell me I'm getting thinner. The 4th of Feb. [John's older sister] Anna's little girl was born. Have today sent some money (papirdollar) to my mother [for his father Bernhard had died in 1894].

13.3 This week I was not well for one day but otherwise everything is fine. In the afternoon my Norwegian friend, Ole Albertsen, and I took a tour to a railway station quite nearby – to a man who works with frames and who was framing photos. The roads were in bad condition and the area was unfamiliar to both of us. We used a wagon. In some place there was no snow and some places the snow was so deep so the trip was fun and quite romantic for us. When we finally came to the right place we met a fellow worker who was proposing marriage to the farmer's beautiful daughter. Yes, last night I was at a dance here in Slocum just so that you know it.

20.3 The mill was shut Thursday, so after work I headed home and was fortunate to get all the way to Shelby (Michigan) where I met Carrie and William, who on Friday morning left for Sparta. On Friday I left together with George and the pastor who left at the same time and I was together with him until we returned on Monday morning

21.3 Saturday morning, it rained a great deal but today the weather is nice. Yesterday morning we had a very cold wind. Auntie burnt her hand today.

[Carrie, George, William mentioned here were John's cousins]

22.3 I came back to Slocum last night and have today worked ¼ day. The saw was finally stopped, so now it is rather uncertain what happens until the new saw arrives. Yesterday morning, it was extremely cold. I'm in good health and expecting a letter from Norway.

27.3 This week I have hardly done any work. Went on Thursday morning to Nathan Pierce's and stayed with them until last evening and enjoyed it. It was a very nice place and people very friendly. Tomorrow it seems the sawing begins again which is good. I am very tired of being idle. Yesterday was extremely cold with a cold wind in the morning.

[John's cousin, Carrie, was married to Nathan Pierce.]

3.4 Easter Day

Henrik Monson and I went today from Slocum to the Swedish church on the other side of Gooding, about 10 miles. We were at Nathan Pierce's for dinner and we went back at 4 o'clock. I worked on Maundy Thursday and Good Friday – for the first time in my life. [These were important religious holidays in Norway.]

4.4 The saw mill has not been open this morning as the people went to the polls for "voting" as they call it here, so fortunately, I did not have to work. I have been working this afternoon. I like it here and feel well but am waiting mail from home (Norway) to hear if Adolf is coming in the spring. If he is not coming, then I will go west.

[Adolf was John's younger brother, born in 1886.]

10.4 It has rained much this week. Continue to feel well but waiting for letter from home.

11.4 This week has been terrible. The last few days have been very windy with rain and snow. Yesterday I got a letter from Adolf, but it does not look like he is coming this spring. I'm in good health and I enjoy the time here.

24.4 Working as a timber lifter gets harder and harder each day. This week got some more snow, which melted right away. Thurs, the 21st I got different work to do, I got a job as material counter, and I'm marking indoors in the mill during the nights. The work is exceedingly nice and clean but one has to deal with the fact of being up at night. Hope that it goes well when I get used to it. Can earn more if I also work during the day on Mondays.

1.5 Like the night work better now, although it takes a bit out of me. Have had nicer weather so it looks like we will have a summer after all. The 28th of last month I had a strange dream. I dreamt that I was back home at Jordbraek and that she came there after I had written to her, and I felt like we were formally engaged. It is too bad that things like these are only dreams. I think so much about this that it messes up my head. [I wonder, did he have a girlfriend back home?]

8.5 Last week we were four Norwegians who rented a house and bought what was needed so that we could make our food, but just think of it, when we got to work on Monday evening, the two of them were fired, so they had to go to Muskegon, where they got work and the third one also went with them, so now I am just about homeless as I do not like to go to the boarding house to sleep there but I may go there to get some food and maybe get a place to stay somewhere else. I think that I will have to stop doing this night work, I'm getting so tired of it and I do not sleep well during the day.

22.5 Have the last 14 days felt real well. I like my night work better although I think I will suffer if I keep on with it for too long. Have had to move from my good accommodation house as the people there were leaving. The place I have now is also good but not so roomy (or clean??)

It is still humid and cold so the spring farming will be late, later than it usually is. I feel that it is not more than two weeks ago that things started turning green. I was in Muskegon last Sunday and I saw a lot. Yesterday evening we had a terrible thunderstorm and fearful lightning flashes, which I think caused some damage.

[The writing in this diary was extremely small and hard to decipher. John has either written about his new place, "renslig" which means "clean" or "romslig" which means "roomy".]

29.5 This week the weather has been nice but very cold and humid. I think it will be a poor or at least a late year for the farmers here. The 26th I got a membership in a club called Free Masons, maybe the same as Masonic Lodge back home. I have to pay 70 cents a month but in return I am more or less provided for. In case I should get ill I would be very well looked after. Included in the same amount, I am insured for $1000.00. I have named my youngest brother as benefactor - Broder Jordbrek, address: Skoger Creamery Company, Drammen Norway.

5.6 This week has been very humid, rain with lightning flashes and warm during the day. It seems to be normal here. I have had a terrible toothache, on Friday night I thought I was going crazy. Ugh, the pain will just about lift me up! I might get my teeth fixed on Saturday. 12.6 This week, I have felt well and will likely stay here if I am not getting good news from the west soon. I am going to a big Circus on Monday and out to Nathan Pierce today.

19.6 Was at Barnum Circus on Monday and it was marvelous, in particular it was interesting to see so many, what should I say, unnaturally well-built people. I saw 4 fully developed people who were only 2 feet tall and the one riding a bicycle was exceptional, he jumped about 5 fathoms on the bike and another one was riding down a steep bridge and around in a "barrel looking arrangement" and when he was near the top his head was down and the bicycle above him.

This week I have been working during the day but I think that I might have to start working nights again if I am going to stay here. Nathan Pierce might also have me to work for him.

[John used the word, favner for "fathoms". 1 favn is 6 feet.]

26.6 Have been in good health this week and I have been working 7 days, was price counter yesterday afternoon and that went well.

10.7 There are big celebrations here on July 4th and I got time off until Wednesday evening to go somewhere and the 4th was a Monday. Stayed with my uncle from Saturday evening till Tuesday noon, then I went to Muskegon where I stayed till Wednesday. Then I went up here to work in the afternoon and during the night. Have also worked another ½ day, so I have 5 days this week.

17.7 Worked 7 days this week but the half day I worked yesterday was very hard because it was so very warm and now for a long time have worked nights – so am not used to the heat. Uncle Ludvig died last month.

24.7 Friday night was the last night shift that the saw went which is also why I worked Friday and yesterday, but yesterday afternoon, I got a job (he didn't seem happy with) so I will likely quit here soon and maybe go west. Have been feeling well except for a little headache the last days.

31.7 Have loaded lumber this week and when they have been cutting hardwood I have been picking it up, so it has been okay.

Think I will quit the 10th of August and then go west as it will be only another 3 months' work here, and it is better to go now than when the cold winter is coming.

6.8 Have this week lifted lumber 5 days but last night I quit at Slocum as I was a bit angry and also so I could get ready to go to Minnesota. I'm going there in about 8 days. Hope it will go well and that I will get a good job. At the moment, I am living at Nathan Pierce's until Monday when I will go home and get ready for my trip west.

Left uncle Hartvig's the 15th August 5:50 morning and [got to] Muskegon by boat 7:30 in the evening.

Arrived Grand Haven 9:30 and departed 11;30. It is now 6 in the morning but we have still not arrived. The boat had lost its course so now it is the second time that it stops to investigate. Arrived Milwaukee (Wisconsin) 8 am.

11:20 am now about 70 miles from Minnesota. Better land.

Arrived Kilbourn 3 pm arrived St. Paul 8:40 pm.

17.8 Arrived Lake Park (Minnesota) 5:15 o'clock and from there I went with Bjornstad and stayed with him for the night and arrived at Brekke's farm on the 18th at 9:00 in the morning. (Brekke and his sons had been neighbours of John's family in Skoger back in Norway

1.9 Have not yet had a day of work so it does not look good for the income. Should have started on a job yesterday but it rained. I think maybe it would be easier to get work in town.

25.9 So far I have not had more than 10 working days here in the west, but I like it here. I've had some very bad stomach trouble but am fine now. Henry Brekke will go along on the same threshing rig as me. This fall and in the winter I will go to school.

9.10 Have been threshing this week and everything has gone well but one can't make much money at this.

30.10 Only a week of the threshing left and then I will be going to school instead of travelling around to various places.

20.11 To-morrow morning I will begin school at Aakers Business School and will be living together with John Brekke during the winter. Hope I get good work in the spring after I've spent money for schooling. [Aakers Business School was in Fargo, North Dakota.]

27.11 Have now attended school one week and all goes well, but it is hard many times. We arrange for our own food.

18.12 Have now got a good start at the school, have kept going for a week with book-keeping in addition to English and mathematics. The only important thing now is to get a good job afterwards. Well, soon I will have to prepare for my second Christmas away from home." [1904]

[The last entry in the diary, which by now was likely filled.]

Chapter Thirteen

WESTERING

After holding an auction sale, the Gronvolds loaded an emigrant car with four horses, two cows, a calf, wagons, household goods, feed and some store goods. Three of the four boys, now young men, rode the emigrant car (Henry worked at Miller's Ranch that summer, for paid work was needed to help cover homesteading expenses). Their parents, Maria, Johan, and sister, Dina, took the train to Ray, ND.

Jens described the building process:

> "We bought lumber in Ray and hauled it fifty miles to Ambrose. We made four trips, two loads to a trip, 2000 feet to the load, and each trip took four days. Adolph and I did the hauling and father and Henry did the building. Mother and Dina stayed on a place near Ray while we did the building. We stored our stuff there and there was pasture for the cows. The 24x50-store building and living quarters included warehouse and a barn for the horses and cows. In the first part of September, we were ready for business.
>
> "On the fifteenth day of November, we [were] snowed in. It stormed furiously for four days. No train until Christmas and we were the only ones to get groceries on that train. A heavier locomotive was brought out to get the train back to Flaxton. Then we had no train

INTERIOR AND EXTERIOR OF GRONVOLD STORE[64]

---

64   From very faded old photos in the family collection. Photoshopped by Marlene
      Atkinsen

until March. Father was lucky to get on that train. He stayed in Fertile that winter [likely with his brother, Lars]." *Note: the rail line only reached Ambrose fall 1906.*

"On the north side of the store, there was a twelve-foot high snow bank. We could jump off the snow bank onto the roof of the building. On the first trip to the homestead that spring [1907] the boys were stuck in a snow bank on the seventeenth of May."[65]

* * *

Earlier that spring of 1906, when Grandmother's oldest brothers, Jens and Henry, went looking further west for homesteads in northeast Montana, they travelled by bicycle. *The Sheridan's Daybreak—A Story of Sheridan County and its Pioneers* told their story of how terrific westerly headwinds forced them to go south to Williston. From there they went to Culbertson, where they hired a "locator" who found quarter sections east of Plentywood for Jens, Henry, and Adolph.

Ambrose, then was the end of a branch of the Soo Railroad line. (Another branch of the Soo came up through Portal, Estevan, Weyburn, areas of Saskatchewan I was most familiar with.) A halfway house between Ambrose and Plentywood was Rolson, where my Melby grandparents lived and ran the post office. As Jens went back and forth, he had stayed with the Melbys several times, first when he brought his fiancée, Mathilda Morvig, out to show her the homestead, and later after their July 1, 1908 marriage back in Fertile, MN. Mrs. Melby apologized, for she hadn't realized they were married when she went to put them up again in separate beds.

Jens and Mathilda raised a family of five and farmed near Plentywood, until 1934 when they moved to Seattle to run a fuel business.

Henry married Helen Flaten in 1913. Helen's situation was unique, for she was the first single woman to homestead in that area in 1909.

---

65   Jens's Story of Maria and Johan

Helen's homestead became their family home, and Henry farmed both areas until 1948, when they retired to Renton, Washington. They had two daughters. Their son died in the 1918 flu epidemic. My grandfather related his surprise when they first met Helen and discovered she had attended school held at Jordbraek, John's home back in Norway. She was actually John's distant cousin.

Great-uncle Adolph, remained a bachelor and lived most of his life in Saskatchewan. When I asked my cousin, Larry Hansen, he reported:

> "Adolph followed his parents into Saskatchewan in 1909, for Johan, now sixty years old, was homesteading for the third time. Adolph eventually let the Plentywood land go."

***

Now the man destined to be my grandfather is coming on scene. After completing the business courses, described in the last chapter, he worked for Huntoon, a banker in Moorhead, Minnesota, at a large farm south of Concordia College. That spring of 1905, his job was breaking wild horses.

At last, John's long-expected brother, Adolph left Norway April 6, 1905 and arrived in Moorhead, April 22. By July, Adolph and John bought a small dairy and hauled milk in Fargo, selling 16 quarts for $1.00.

John wrote in his memoir, "The next summer (1906) we sold the milk business- the cows and cow barn and took our four old horses and wagons and got a railroad car with a Mr. Monsen and went to Flaxton, ND. We hauled what we had by wagon from there to Fortuna. We spotted some land and drove to Williston with our old horses to file on the land and bring back some lumber.

Monsen and Adolph got their papers on the land they had spotted but what I had picked was already taken, so we brought back lumber for my brother's little 10'x12' house. We had a small tent we slept in as we built the house. After we built the house we took a plow and made two or three furrows about 30 feet apart and made a fire to burn up the dry grass between the rows of the fire guard. It gave us a trying time when the fire jumped the furrow and the four of us worked for our life to get it out. We were so tired we fell down and slept there several hours."[66]

According to what my uncles, Lloyd and Johnny, told me September 2013, our family might have been born as Americans except for the fact John lost out on that parcel of land he wanted to file on.

John and Adolph worked on a threshing crew at Portal, ND. After threshing was done, they went back to Ambrose, ND, bought a building site where they built a 10x12 house and a barn for their horses. John worked at building a cellar under a large store and later hauled lumber to homesteaders for their shacks. For the winter, he went back to Moorhead to visit with friends from his old home in Skoger, Norway.

The spring of 1907 he went back to Ambrose where he had a cement business. He noticed a lovely Norsk girl, Dina Gronvold, daughter of Johan J. & Maria Gronvold who owned the general store. He got work in a lumber yard and worked his way up to second man, then quit and got a job doing the same work for a big new lumber yard, Kulaas Lumber. [A panoramic picture on www.AmbroseND.com website reveals three lumberyards.]

John became their agent, moving into the living quarters beside the office. How busy it was in those first years, with many homesteaders crowding into the area west and north across the forty-ninth parallel into southern Saskatchewan. Many nights his "office" floor filled with men resting up for the return trip back to their claims.

***

How was that first ember of interest in my grandmother generated? My grandfather, John wrote in his memoir that Dina's voice was the first point of attraction as he sat in front of her at a church service in Ambrose's railroad station.

---

66   J.B. Hansen's personal memoir written in the 1950's in an old ledger book. In 1972, on a trip to visit their first grandchildren, born on the same day, my mother and her sister, Clara, spent the ten-hour car trip translating from Norwegian to English. Later Clara wrote out and photocopied this translation

Singing hymns was something they did for a pastime in those pre-radio or TV days. Dina said, "In the winter time we used to sit around the table singing hymns, one after another. Mother was a good singer."

Practice makes perfect!

John started taking Dina out. In the summer of 1908 they went by buggy all the way to Plentywood, Montana to visit her three brothers who had homesteaded there.

> An article titled *Ambrose, the Queen City of Divide County from November 1911* boasted:
>
> "Ambrose is known as the greatest little city in the state. It is the terminus of the Flaxton branch of the Soo railway, fifty-eight miles in length... surrounded by a rich agricultural territory, the resources of which have tended to make the city a thriving market for both American and Canadian grain. The village of Ambrose was founded in the fall of 1906 and was incorporated as such in the spring of 1907 and incorporated as a city in the spring of 1911, a title which it has well earned."
>
> This article appeared in the November 4, 1911 *Fargo Forum,* and appeared again the next week in the Ambrose paper. The article went on to list an impressive number of businesses for such a new place. But the website[67] where I learned this said Ambrose was on its way to becoming the ghost town it is now, as a result of a 1913 fire and the effects of the thirties.
>
> Erling Ebbeson, writing of the 1906-1916 period, gave me this interesting glimpse of

---

67   www.AmbroseND.com http://www.ambrosend.com/42-ebbeson_erling.html taken from pages 53-55 of the *Divide County History 1974,* Crosby, North Dakota

my grandmother:"Also I seem to recall a Mr. Gronvold having a store and eating place on the northwest corner of the Miller intersection. Among other things he sold corn flakes called Egg-O-See. A salesman came in one morning and asked if they had corn flakes and the waitress, a comely young Scandinavian gal, replied, "Eg go see", and so a name was born"[68]

***

Both my mother and father's families homesteaded in Southern Saskatchewan, ten miles north of the border and the same distance from each other. As a child, I thought my mother's and father's American cousins were better off than we were. I wondered what forces had been in play that brought about my grandparents' move across the forty-ninth parallel, making me Canadian.

When I learned about the extensive collections of published and unpublished documents and photographs related to the history of Western Canada held at the Glenbow, I went to search out material to answer those unanswerable questions. A few hours spent at the Archives in Calgary's Glenbow Museum revealed aspects of Canada's immigration policy and history previously unknown to me. As the nineteenth century ended and the first decades of the twentieth began, an active movement of Canada's national parliament encouraged American homesteaders to move across the line to Canada. A book titled *Only Farmers Need Apply* described this plan.[69]

The Canadian government employed a variety of methods to influence American homesteaders to go north. Editors and correspondents were brought to Canada by the trainload to see "the land of opportunity" at Government expense, in return for writing promotional newspaper

---

68   As above

69   Harold Martin Troper, <u>Only Farmers Need Apply</u>- Official Canadian
      Government Encouragement of Immigration from the United States 1896-1911
      Griffin House 1972 192 pp

articles. Local fairs featured exhibits of Canadian produce. Promotional meetings, lectures or parties, where the state agent followed up on mail-outs (or chain letters) were all methods engaged as an efficient way of getting names of those interested in homesteading in the opening Canadian West.

ALL NIGHT IN LINE AT DOMINION LANDS OFFICE SETTLING ESTEVAN SASK.

WE THINK THE FOURTH PERSON TO THE RIGHT OF THE CORNER WAS J.B. HANSEN

Since American immigrants already knew about prairie conditions and the necessary farming techniques, they were highly desired. The common thought was that they had a fair level of financial backing.

Ethnic and/or religious groups formed the base for many Canadian prairie settlements—yet it was shocking to realize that some groups were negatively referred to as riff-raff, for the policy ruled out some religious, ethnic, and racial groups. My Norwegian ancestors were among the immigrant groups looked on favourably by the department. The Interior Department was also responsible for creating pockets of ethnic settlements across Western Canada. Norwegians and Jews predominated in the area where I grew up. When my mother taught school in the 1930s, the classroom in her home district was divided evenly between both groups.

***

The fall of 1908, John filed on a homestead land and preemption in Saskatchewan, Canada, and he filed by proxy for his brother, Adolph. Johan and Olaf Gronvold filed on land next to his. I remember hearing that when John made the journey across the border from Ambrose up to Estevan on September 16, 1908, they camped out on the sidewalk on the southeast corner of Fourth Street and Twelfth Avenue in order to be at the front of the line when the Homesteading Office opened.

That fall, his brothers-in-law to be, Henry & Jens hauled lumber up out of Plentywood, Montana for John's 12x16 homestead shack. A 12x12 kitchen and sleeping area was added later as the family increased.

***

From the time after she left Fertile, Minnesota, Dina saved a collection of postcards received mostly from her cousins from three different families back in Minnesota—including one I was glad to discover, from her older cousin, Jenny. One postcard shown on AmbroseND.com (one Dina might have sent) showed a postman with his sack giving a girl a hug with this caption, "You are far away from Ambrose ND, but I haven't forgotten you."

Postcards had just become common. The messages were brief—these were my Grandma's equivalent to the text messages of today. There appeared to be discussion alluding to a love interest in her life; Dina seems shy about any details until there are congratulatory messages after her marriage. And a card from her brother Henry indicates that Dina and her family might have been sick or in quarantine just before the wedding.

***

An Ambrose newspaper clipping she saved from March 1909 reported:

> "John Hansen, manager of Kulaas Lumber Yard, was united in marriage to Miss Dina Gronvold, daughter of one of our leading merchants, at the Gronvold home on Tuesday evening of this week. The affair was a very quiet one, only a few of the most intimate friends having any knowledge of it. Mr. and Mrs. Hansen will reside in Ambrose."

But not for long. By the 1909 spring breakup, John and Dina had moved to the Saskatchewan homestead. There was no end of work to begin. To satisfy requirements for their claim, they must live there for at least six months of the year, break a certain amount of land each year, and become Canadian citizens, all within the subsequent five years.

The town of Tribune, SK was about eight miles northeast of their Canadian homestead. Until the railroad reached Tribune in 1913, my grandfather made the long thirty-mile trip southeast back to Ambrose to sell his crops and buy supplies. This was done with horse and wagon over prairie trails, not developed roads. Such trips necessitated John's absence for at least a night or two.

***

Johan and Maria Gronvold, my great-grandparents, also moved that same year to their homestead NE 25-2-15-W2 where they built their store. All through the years, the family referred to that land as "Grandma's

Grandma, wearing the same elaborate hat she had as part of her wedding outfit, is in the centre of this community picture holding my mother as a baby. Grandfather, JB Hansen is to her left. My other grandfather, Dahl Melby is the second man on the left side.

Quarter" although it was shared with her brother, Adolph—they each farmed half.

A year later, they moved the store building a mile or so southwest by stoneboats (a flat sledge, so named, as they were used for transporting stones). The homestead of Dina's younger brother, Olaf, neighboured John and Dina's to the northeast. Since good water was there, this was where they operated the store.

My cousin, Larry Hansen, said that he and [Uncle] Bernhard went one day to look at the old store building that was still in Nick's yard against the west trees until the late seventies. It wasn't very big. It was not much more than a ten-minute walk northeast across the prairie for my grandmother, Dina, to visit her mother, Maria, after my mother, Edith Marie, Maria's first grandchild, was born in March 1910.

Within a few years, Johan acquired a half section near Ratcliffe (likely when Olaf married Christine Gjelten in 1913). Their new place was three miles southwest of the Hansen family homestead starting into the hills. Johan and Maria lived there until they passed away. Adolph made his home with them, acquiring the place when his parents passed away—Maria in 1928, and Johan in 1930. Both were eighty-one years of age at their death. Canada was their home for the last quarter of their life while Norway had been their first.

During this period of transitions and early development, and through all the years up to the early fifties, the Gronvold family members stayed in close touch.

And John and Dina's busy and expanding family crowded the two-room homestead shack. Dina's few treasures were packed away for safe-keeping, among them the Princess Doll.

ISSUED BY DIRECTION OF HON. SYDNEY FISHER
MINISTER OF AGRICULTURE, OTTAWA, CANADA.

GLENBOW ARCHIVES 971-2-C212C-1909[70]. THE
INTERIOR DEPARTMENT OF THE CANADIAN GOVERNMENT
PUBLISHED BROCHURES FOR MAIL-OUT. TITLES LIKE *THE
LAST BEST WEST, THE WONDROUS WEST* OR *THE LAND
OF OPPORTUNITY*, CREATED A GLOWING PICTURE OF THE
COUNTRY OF CANADA AND PROVIDED USEFUL INFORMATION
ABOUT CARRYING ON THE JOB OF FARMING IN CANADA.

---

70   http://ww2.glenbow.org/search/archivesPhotosResults.aspx?XC=/search/
      archivesPhotosResults.aspx&TN=IMAGEBAN&AC=QBE_QUERY&RF=WebRes
      ults&DF=WebResultsDetails&DL=0&RL=0&NP=255&MR=10&QB0=AND&Q
      F0=File%20number&QI0=971-2-c212c-1909

Chapter Fourteen

THE LAST BEST WEST

In Retrospect

The number of vehicles in the Hansen yard indicated an important event. Around sixty Hansen cousins, their spouses, children, and our remaining aunts and uncles gathered for a family celebration on October 3, 2009. Our grandparent's homestead was a 100-year-old farm. The previous winter, the Saskatchewan Provincial Government had acknowledged century farms with a special ceremony.

My cousin, Brad, his wife Kelly, and three sons, who operate the farm, hosted us at the old home place. This event was a suitable launch for my planned ten-day family history trip, retracing my great grandparent's and grandparent's immigrant journey.

The circle of much-loved familiar faces standing around that memorable old kitchen, along with the aroma of coffee, welcomed me. Continuing into the next room, historical pictures and documents were spread over the large old oval dining room table. It once accommodated the original Hansen family of twelve. Now, Princess, my silent travelling partner for the historical trip, shared space with family memorabilia recent in comparison with her.

Too soon, the call went out to gather outside. The south of the house had been the location for many a celebratory picture over the past 100 years. The afternoon's few short hours of sharing were ending. One of the proudest to be here where he had farmed for so many years was our ninety-four-year-old Uncle Clarence along with his wife, Vera.

Brad and Kelly, celebrating a better-than-average harvest that year, provided a catered supper for all of us at the Tribune Hall, extending our time together. Brad explained the intricacies of modern farming with GPS, fascinating to a former farm girl familiar with fifties grain farming.

Moreover, the assembled Hansen tribe, true to their heritage, appreciated the good food and the opportunity to celebrate such a significant milestone in our family's history.

The Princess Doll made an appearance at the program while I struggled with the emotion of expressing what grandmother's gift had meant to me, and how that inspired this journey that became *The Princess Doll's Scrapbook*.

My uncle Johnny spoke a few words on behalf of the senior generation. Like my grandfather before him, he would not fail to remind us of the importance of our Christian faith.

Our Richest Heritage

The blissful union of body, soul and mind
creates a seed of infinite value.
For contained therein—a heart, soul, body and
mind—love breathed, heaven has spoken.

Once claim to a name above all other names
and bought with a price beyond earthly treasure—
God's spirit indwells and His glory swells
out into a seeking world.

This cycle does not end so long as one tends
to the journey Love has spoken.
And each little spark God uses as a part
of His greater plan to gather the nations.

As generations pass, a torch is passed
from spirit to spirit to spirit,
And each claim to the name brings glory and
inflames other burned-out candles.

Let us be thankful for our part in this chain—
for forefathers who believed,
received, and passed along
our richest heritage.

As each of us go home, Joy will be unsurpassed
by any but love as we worship at Jesus'
feet and pray for those
on their journey to come.[71]

***

71   Written by my niece, Nicole Melby Frank, used with permission.

A wedding invitation for my niece's wedding on June 30, 2012 was to be my first trip back to Saskatchewan since that 100th commemoration. I was determined that, besides taking in the celebration, I would visit my aunt Evelyn, whose health had failed terribly since I last sat with her at the homestead anniversary. I would also visit the place Maria lived in the final quarter of her life.

As I entered the church for the Saturday morning wedding, news quietly being shared was that our dear aunt Evelyn, the last of the five Hansen sisters, had passed away late the night before.

We celebrated new beginnings and a life of promise for Danielle and Davis.

Then, the next week, her big extended circle of family and friends celebrated Evelyn's life—and the promise of eternal life—as a number of her nieces and nephews sang "What a day that will be, when my Jesus I shall see."

After the forty-mile funeral procession from Estevan, we met at the Dravland Cemetery for the burial. A work bee had tidied up the prairie grass and got it ready, for we not only laid Evelyn to rest, we revisited the final resting places of five generations of the family, starting with Johan and Maria.

***

On a hilltop, two miles to the southwest of the cemetery, I could see Maria and Johan's house again. My visit there the day before gave me the opportunity to wander around and wonder about Maria's experiences there.

The house still stands erect, though it hasn't been occupied since my great uncle Adolph lived there in the fifties. Barn swallows inhabit the windowless living room, facing toward the southeast. An interesting eight-sided granary to the east of the house is starting to collapse in upon itself. The kitchen room on the west side still had a portable free-standing kitchen cupboard standing amongst the rubble of crumbled plaster ceiling.

ELAINE MELBY AYRE

Narrow stairs wound around the chimney to two upstairs sleeping areas. I had to turn my foot sideways to fit each riser. How could Maria manage them? A chimney cover at the top of the stairs indicated a small space heater had once been in use there. Other than pink plaster chunks, there was also an old trunk, likely Johan's emigrant trunk.

***

The barn roof, reddened by years of exposure, had buckled in on itself. Below the barn, an accumulation of assorted metal scrap included an old wood stove.

"Now this must be Maria's stove!" I exclaimed.

Jens's story told about Maria's only sibling to remain in Norway:

"Syverine was the only one left in Norway. She married Per Anton Gamsveen. When Syverine died, the nurse, who took care of her, married Per Anton, expecting to get the farm, but she was disappointed. Per Anton deeded the farm to a youth organization. In 1903, Maria received a forty dollar inheritance. That's when she got a new cook stove which lasted till 1940."

Beyond the yard, to the southwest was a prairie slough. I thought it was important that Maria could see water, for her home in Norway was within 500 meters of a river and lake. Here, she could see flocks of ducks return each spring, and come to appreciate the Saskatchewan seasons.

MARIA'S STOVE

THE TREES FROM THE HANSEN HOMESTEAD IS
ON THE HORIZON TO THE NORTHEAST

This Princess-inspired journey did satisfy my curiosity, but only partially. As one question was answered, it led to another, then another. Via the internet, I connected with fourth-cousins and cousins of cousins, and those people fascinated with the game of uncovering history; it became an all-consuming passion with always one more question!

It wasn't just Maria's North American arrival on that 1869 date that so compelled me—it was the framework of all the happenings within her family group from the time before and after her birth.

The phrase from the Apostle's Creed, "I believe in the communion of saints," I've often repeated in church. Now that I have learned about and shared the challenges and frustrations these "saints" experienced, it has brand-new meaning and encouragement. I remembered the time I discovered I was pregnant at age forty-three and realized, to my comfort, that this had also been Maria's experience, as well as her mother before, and her daughter later.

Yet, many aspects of their lives I could not begin to know, for:

> "The determination of early immigrants is almost incomprehensible today, as is their lack of complaint... Who found the courage to keep going on because there was no going home again. Whose language, religion, culture often marginalized them for a generation.

> "...There is something magnificent about the small people [like my Maria] who wandered through our history unaccounted for, who had the gumption and grit to move blindly toward a promise and to keep their disappointments to themselves."[72]

As I studied the doll's face—the delicate pursed lips, the slightly dreamy, almost pensive eyes, I wondered, "What can she tell me?"

Those of my family's first generation in America (first Jenny and Nelly, then Ragna and my grandmother, Dina, along with her special cousins,

---

72   © LindaLee Tracey, *A Scattering of Seeds*, McArthur & Company, Toronto, 1999. Published with permission

Malla, Clara, and Nora, who all must have played with Princess) surely thought she was special. Maria, who I thought had picked her out did, and I did, too. I felt compelled to share what she inspired so the succeeding generations, family or not, could be part of an emigration/immigration story, written because of a doll, so out of the ordinary; she was called Princess.

"For now we see only a reflection as in a mirror;
Then we shall see face to face.
Now I know in part;
Then I shall know fully,
Even as I am fully known.

And now these three remain:
Faith, hope and love.
But the greatest of these is love."[73]

---

73   1 Corinthians 13: 12,13 (New International Version)

Acknowledgements

I want to acknowledge my thanks to God: for His many gifts, for His guidance, for being part of this family and for those ah-ha moments throughout the development of this story as I became aware, again and again of how my life experiences had been a part of God's Gracious plan.

Thank you to my husband, Gary Ayre, for his patience with the countless hours I've spent on the computer and his ongoing support and encouragement.

As I started my writing journey with the Institute for Children's Literature, Clara Gillow Clark mentored me and wisely advised me to do my book as non-fiction, all via snail mail.

Then this book took shape online through the lessons of the Advanced Writing course with Kristi Collier Thompson as my ICL instructor for three quarters of the course. She kept me on track, avoiding rabbit trails! Linda Brennan, took over on the last two lessons when the book came together in one manuscript and helped me finish strong.

Philip Ramstad, a fourth cousin I have never met, except via the internet, has been my biggest cheerleader. I thank him for his kind comments that are on the book cover. He provided information about the members of my great grandmother's maternal family. He and his wife, Lucy read my manuscripts countless times, gave advice and encouragement.

Garth Ulrich, another fourth cousin, answered many questions. The extensive family tree he researched gave me the overall picture of Maria's paternal family.

My cousin, Larry Hansen, our resident Hansen family historian answered many questions. He was responsible for posting our Hansen family tree and family pictures on Ancestry.com — a great help on this project.

Barb Raaen went out of her way to research in Minnesota records for this story.

Gary Krahenbuhl, Henry Olds and Loyd Erion provided information about the Espe family.

Maggie Land Blanck's wonderful emigration/immigration website helped me understand what Maria and her sister and brother experienced that day they landed on America's shores. Thanks for providing 300dpi pictures to illustrate the Doll's Scrapbook

Norway Heritage Website and its webmaster, Borge Solem provided images for which rights were paid. Other sources were Library of Congress, New York Public Library, Glenbow Museum and Archives, and CanStock Images.

Marlene Atkinsen assisted in preparing a number of the images for the book and in the process we became friends, sharing our common interest in writing.

Thanks to everyone mentioned here as well as to my friends and Facebook friends and to family who provided encouragement and kept me believing this book was possible. It's been a long process.

And finally, my thanks to you, dear reader. I pray this book will be a blessing to you.

PHOTO CREDITS: LIZ WOODS MILESTONE MOMENTS

About the Author

As the oldest daughter of the oldest daughter of one of the early homesteading families from Souris Valley RM No. 7 in southeastern Saskatchewan, Elaine was always interested in the history of her immigrant grandparents but never imagined she would write about it.

Being gifted with her grandmother's old and damaged porcelain doll inspired a lifelong search for answers about the doll and its place in the family. Finally when her granddaughter was born she determined to write a story about the doll. Writing courses taken through the Institute for Children's Literature prepared her for the task. The Doll's Scrapbook was started as a nonfiction book to make use of the quantity of research material she had accumulated.

A retired Home Economics teacher, Elaine still works as a part-time cook at a local senior's lodge, volunteers as a board member of the local Adult Learning Society, likes reading, gardening, and crafts, though crafts and sewing projects have taken a back seat since she started writing.

Elaine and her husband have three grown sons and two grandchildren and enjoy country life on their central Alberta acreage with a few of their remaining Canadian Horses, and their dog, Molly.